How
Retire Young

Other "One Hour Guides"

How to Retire Young

Edward M. Tauber

DOW JONES-IRWIN
Homewood, Illinois 60430

Project editor: Jane Lightell
Production manager: Ann Cassady
Cover design: Image House
Cover illustration: David Lesh
Compositor: Carlisle Communications, Ltd.
Typeface: 11/13 Century Schoolbook
Printer: Arcata Graphics/Kingsport

Library of Congress Cataloging-in-Publication Data

Tauber, Edward, 1943–
    How to retire young.

    Bibliography: p.
    Includes index.
    1. Early retirement—United States—Planning.
I. Title.
HD7110.5.U6T38   1989   332.024'01   88–25748
ISBN 1-55623-153-9 (pbk.)

Printed in the United States of America
    2 3 4 5 6 7 8 9 0 K 6 5 4 3 2 1 0 9

PREFACE

This is *not* a book on how to get rich quick. It is *not* a book of investment advice. It *is* a book to help those with average or above-average income plan and achieve early retirement by age 55 to 45 or younger. To achieve this goal, the reader need not be brilliant or lucky. He need only plan his career and develop saving and investment habits using all the early retirement oriented tools available to him. No magic. No high risk. It's the same way millions of Americans retire now—only they start too late; they cannot afford to retire until they're in their mid-60s.

Early retirement can be an event, but it can also be a state of mind. It's the financial freedom to do what you want without pressure. Continue your job, start a second career, take a sabbatical, travel, enjoy sports and hobbies, or do whatever you want to do. When you retire early, you make your own time truly your own.

TAKE THE HIGH ROAD

Throughout this book you will find a consistent philosophy expressed: Take the high road. That is, follow the path with the highest odds of success. Many books have been written offering advice on every area of career planning, retirement planning, saving, and investment. There are as many points of view as there are books. Much of the advice is oriented toward the quick buck, taking paths that often have a very low probability of success. In short, you might as well play the lottery.

There is no best way for everyone. But there are paths to success that have reasonable odds based on history. The recommendations in this book attempt to guide you to an early retirement with as close to a sure bet as possible. If you are a gambler by nature, you may find the prescriptions here too time-consuming and methodical. But gamblers lose as well as win. No one can afford to gamble and lose their retirement. Take the high road.

CONTENTS

Worksheet. Example Using The Worksheet.
Making It Simpler. What If I Save Ten
Percent.

CHAPTER 9 Save Early, Save More, Save Smart 59

When Your Money Works For You, You Don't
Have To Work For Your Money. Save Early.
Save More. Save With A Carrot. Credit Rich,
Saving Poor. Save Smart. Let Uncle Sam Save
For You. Shelter Interest From Taxes. Let
Your Employer Contribute. You Can Have It
Now And Later. Annual Spending Worksheet.
Save Two Pools of Money. Investing Smart.
Seek Advice And Manage Your Investments.
A Winning Strategy To Beat The Market.

CHAPTER 10 The Tools of Early Retirement 73

IRA: The Do It Yourself Pension. Who Can
Save. Invest In What. Harvesting The IRA
Early. Tax-Deferred Annuities. Single
Premium Life Insurance. Company Plans.
401(K). Simplified Employee Pension. Pension
Plans. Defined Contribution and Defined
Benefit Plans. 403(b). Keogh. Military And
Civil Service. Ask Now. Questions To Ask
About Your Pension.

CHAPTER 11 The Wrong Side of Forty 89

The Advantages. Greater Returns Can Make
The Difference. A Sample Plan.

How to Retire Young

CHAPTER 1

YOU CAN RETIRE YOUNG

Early retirement can be achieved and can be wonderful. Retirement means having the financial freedom to do what you want—to play golf and tennis, to travel, to start a second career, to teach, to write a book, or maybe just to take a sabatical from the routine of life. Many people do experience a midlife crisis in their 40s and get burned out with their work. However, if you no longer need that income, you have a choice. Just the state of mind that you can stay, quit, or do whatever is a tremendous uplift. What you do everyday should be challenging and fun. But if you're working just to cover next month's mortgage, work can be a prison.

The premise of this book is that many people can retire early, it's simply a matter of dedication and planning.

RETIREMENT IS WASTED ON THE OLD

Think of life as having three periods: schooling, working, and savoring. Many of us spend the first twenty-five years of life in school, work for forty years, and retire at age 65, only to savor the last ten or so. Why not plan life in three equal installments: schooling for 25 years, working for 25 years, and savoring for 25. If you could do it, there are some big pluses. Although men at age 65 have a further life expectancy of 14 years and women 18 years, many do not live that long. Everyone has heard a story about the guy who saved all his life, retired at 65, and dropped dead at 66. Also, you hear how wonderful life can be at 70. But let's face it, most 70 year olds don't have the energy to enjoy things the way they did at 50. Travel and exercise are tougher. Health problems are much more prevalent. Even if you are in good shape, friends are in poor health, hospitalized, or dying! If you had a choice, wouldn't you rather spend your retirement years in your 50s or younger? If youth is wasted on the young, retirement is wasted on the old.

ALLOCATION OF LIFETIME INCOME

Imagine that you have a fixed amount of income to spend over your life. When do you want to spend it? You can live well when you are middle-aged, work longer, and let that money earn compound interest and be wealthy at age 65. Or you can live modestly, save, and spend more between 45 and 65. This is a critical question everyone should address but few consider. Most early retirees believe that they will gain more enjoyment from spending a larger part of their lifetime income in the middle years. It's like this: would you rather have an income of $50,000 at age 55 and an inflation adjusted income of $30,000 at 75 or vice versa? The answer to that question demonstrates whether you believe you will enjoy money more in your earlier years or in your later years. If you are convinced that a 25-year or longer retirement period makes sense for you, then you need to plan now to make it happen.

BUT I DON'T WANT TO RETIRE

You may not want to retire early. You might even think retirement at anytime sounds awful: being put out to pasture, out of the mainstream, over the hill, just waiting to die. The reason most people think this negatively about retirement is because most retirees are old! But retirement can be something totally different if you retire when you're young.

According to the American Association of Retired Persons (AARP), the largest organization (23 million members) representing people over 50, retirement means:

"Embarking on a new and vital phase of life, one filled with fresh opportunities, expanded interests, new friends, and deep satisfaction."[1]

This does not sound like the typical stereotype of the bitter dropout, the forlorn aged, the obsolete castaway, or the lost soul waiting for God's call. Yet, retirement has typically been a negative concept from the vantage point of the young or middle aged, as if it's something we all must *face* someday rather than something we can look forward to.

However retiring young is something different. It's a second chance, a new life, a redirection, to play without time pressure, and work without financial pressure. Retiring young is the American dream, and more and more people are aiming for it and succeeding.

THE WORKING RETIRED

If you do not want to retire—fine. Would you like to start your own business someday? Would you like to change careers? Would you like to go to work in an area of the country where you cannot get a job now? Would you like to continue your present career, but under a lot less pressure?

These are the types of things that the working retired do. When you have the means to support yourself and your family, you can start a new business, job, or career without being under the same gun that you are when this month's paycheck just pays this month's bills. The freedom of early retirement allows you to explore and study what you would like to do with your life rather than to simply react to whatever immediate options you face.

Your earnings from working after retirement are different also. Since you have covered your expenses with income from pensions, savings, and so on, working income can be used as fun money. You can buy the things you want because all of this

---

[1]"Planning Your Retirement." *AARP,* 1986, p. 1

income is discretionary. No wonder more people are opting for early retirement.

EARLY RETIREMENT IS "IN"

In January 1979, Congress initiated the Age Discrimination In Employment Act which prohibited companies from forcing an employee to retire at 65 simply because of his or her age. Despite this change which allowed workers to continue working, most do not!

Charles D. Spencer & Associates conducted a study of retirees in 1986 who had pension plans with large companies. Similar studies in 1978 revealed 62 percent of workers retired before age 65. In 1986 the figure rose to a whopping 84 percent. Only 5 percent of retirees in 1986 were age 65, 3 percent were above 65, and the remainder were disability cases. Spencer found less than two of every 1000 workers were over 65. In fact, almost one-third of the nation's males age 55 to 64 have left the labor force! The early retirement trend has begun. (See Figure 1–1)

THE AFFORDABILITY OF EARLY RETIREMENT: AN ILLUSTRATION FROM THE TYPICAL CENSUS FAMILY

You are no doubt asking yourself: How can I do it on my income? A hypothetical example points to why this author believes many people can do it if they have the motivation. The median household income in the United States is about $24,000. However, those age 25 to 34 have incomes of $25,000 and those 35 to 44 have $31,000. The peak earning years are 45 to 54 at $33,000. Median incomes drop back down to the mid-20,000s between ages 55 to 64. Today the median household income of the traditional retiree group age 65 to 74 is a modest $15,000. Let's look at this hypothetical median census household who wants to save enough *by age 55* to make the median retirement salary of $15,000 or more. As a goal to generate $15,000 a year at 55, if this household starts at age 25, how much do they need to

FIGURE 1–1
Share of Men Not in Work Force

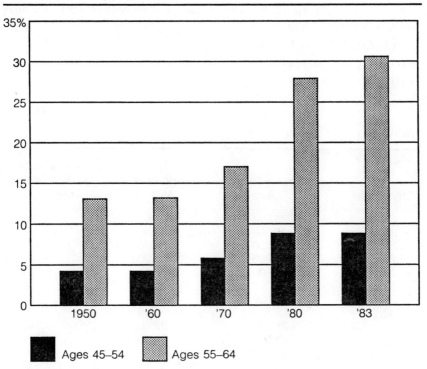

Source: U.S. Dept. of Labor.

save each year? They could achieve this goal by saving $3,577 a year, which assumes a real 5 percent return (e.g. 10 percent interest less 5 percent inflation). Thus, if they saved this much annually they would save $588,458, which could produce a 25-year retirement income stream of $64,829 a year, which at their age of 55 would be equal to $15,000 today.

Now maybe it would be tough to save that much in the early periods of their career. They might save less then, but more after age 35 and even more after 45 when their peak earning power goes up and inflation can help them save even more. Let's look at it step-by-step to demonstrate what would happen if they saved just 10 percent of their gross income in a tax-deferred retirement account every year for the next 30 years.

Remember they make $25,000 from age 25 to 34, $31,000 from age 35 to 44, and $33,000 from age 45 to 54, retiring at age 55. We assume they save 10 percent of salary and can earn a true return of 5 percent. A true return is the return above the level of inflation. If inflation is 5 percent, they would have to earn 10 percent each year—a reasonable objective with conservative investments (see Table 1–1).

TABLE 1–1

Their Age	Income in Today's Dollars	10% Saved Annually	Value at Their Age 55 at a True 5% Return
25	25,000	2,500	10,805
26	25,000	2,500	10,290
27	25,000	2,500	9,800
28	25,000	2,500	9,334
29	25,000	2,500	8,889
30	25,000	2,500	8,466
31	25,000	2.500	8,063
32	25,500	2,500	7,679
33	25,000	2,500	7,313
34	25,000	2,500	6,965
35	31,000	3,100	8,225
36	31,000	3,100	7,833
37	31,000	3,100	7,461
38	31,000	3,100	7,105
39	31,000	3,100	6,767
40	31,000	3,100	6,445
41	31,000	3,100	6,138
42	31,000	3,100	5,846
43	31,000	3,100	5,567
44	31,000	3,100	5,302
45	33,000	3,300	5,375
46	33,000	3,300	5,119
47	33,000	3,300	4,876
48	33,000	3,300	4,643
49	33,000	3,300	4,422
50	33,000	3,300	4,212
51	33,000	3,300	4,011
52	33,000	3,300	3,820
53	33,000	3,300	3,638
54	33,000	3,300	3,465

Total Dollars Saved equals $89,000

Value of total savings plus interest at age 55 equals $197,874

This total savings of 198,000 would produce a fixed income of $20,990 a year for 30 years (age 56 to 85) at 10 percent interest earned on money.

Since we have already allowed for inflation, this annual income is stated in today's dollars.

Now, you may think, "*I* could not retire on $21,000 a year at 55, especially since any additional income from Social Security would not be available until age 62." There are three reasons you may do better:

This median census household never increased its percentage of income saved during the higher earning years of 45 to 55. At this age most of us have more discretionary income, so saving 15 percent or more is possible.

Also, this census household had very small *real* raises in income. The hypothetical family had one raise of 24 percent, but only after 10 years! The second raise after the next 10 years was just 6 percent. You will have better raises!

Finally, this median census household received only $24,000 to $33,000 during its working years. You may make a lot more. For example, if your income is over $50,000 you can save a lot more. The higher your income, the more of it is discretionary, thus you should be able to save a greater *percentage* of it.

IS IT TOO LATE?

How long does it take to achieve this goal once you begin? Some of the early retirees interviewed in this book did it in 10 years. The author decided to *begin* working for retirement at age 37 and succeeded in six years, retiring at age 43. If you are in your mid-20s to mid-40s you have time to work for the goal of retiring young.

IF YOU ARE 40 NOW YOU CAN STILL DO IT

It is not impossible. If you want a pretax income of $30,000 at age 55, in today's terms that means $62,370 a year income 15 years from now when you turn 55 (at an assumed inflation rate of 5 percent). How much will you have to save by age 55 to generate $62,370 per year over a twenty-five year retirement if it could earn 10 percent? Answer: $566,130. Thus, if you could save $566,000 by age 55 you could draw a fixed income of $62,000 throughout your assumed life expectancy of 25 years (to age 80). In today's dollars, this would be the equivalent of $30,000 at age 55, $18,000 at age 65, and $11,000 at age 75. This fixed-payment schedule assumes that your financial needs will be lower as you grow older and Medicare and Social Security begin.

How can you get $566,000 at age 55 if you have no savings now? If you can earn 10 percent on any future savings, how much do you have to put away each year to reach this goal 15 years from now? Answer: $17,820. For many professional people, entrepreneurs, or two-income households, this is *do-able*. And, you can take advantage of the variety of tax-shelter retirement plans that the government offers to save this money pretax. This will be explained later. If you have some savings in the appreciation of your home, vested pension benefits, or money in financial assets, you need to save even less.

Now, what if you are age 45 and only have 10 years to achieve your goal? To have a $30,000 per year income, you have to save $28,000 a year. If you are 35, you need only put away $13,000 a year or $9,000 if you're now age 30. These calculations are rather conservative. They assume that you will make only 10 percent on your investments. If you can average 12 to 14 percent in stocks or 2nd trust deeds, you can achieve your goal faster than 10 to 15 years. You can also achieve your goal faster if you can adjust your lifestyle to live on a lesser retirement income or if you can save more in future years.

You may still be thinking, "How can I save this much?" Even if you make enough income to save it, aftertax savings are expensive. This book will review these issues and offer clues how those who retired early used their expertise and the tax laws to help them do it.

If you want to retire early, there are no magic formulas. It requires hard work to make money and requires smart work to learn how to save on a pretax basis. If you invested 15 to 20 years in school to learn how to make money, why not spend a little effort to plan how to capitalize on your earning power to be able to enjoy it for a third of your life on your terms in early retirement?

In this book, a number of topics will be covered to help you decide if it's worth it to you to set up a plan to retire early:

- Life After Work—How To Savor It
- Retirement In Baby-Boom America: Year 2010–2030
- Managing Your Career
- The Four Steps To Early Retirement
- Simplified Lifestyles—The Key To Retirement Living
- Setting Goals—How Much Do You Need
- How To Save Smart
- Tools of Early Retirement
- Ten Who Did It

CHAPTER 2

IS THERE LIFE AFTER WORK?

Many people are not sure they really want to retire early. Early retirement may sound good at first, but then you ask—What would I do with all that free time? Who would I be without my work? Why should I even get up in the morning? The first step in planning to retire early is to make certain that that is what *you* want to do.

BORN TO WORK

In America, the Protestant ethic runs deep throughout the culture. We are born to work. Work is good for its own sake. Work is its own reward. To be out of work is a black mark. When you meet someone new they often ask "and what do you do?" The only expected answer is your occupation, your job, how you earn money. They would be shocked if you said, "I raise roses, I play golf, or I do something different every day." Society as a whole is likewise oriented to work. We read everyday in newspapers about the trends in the gross national product. Is the country producing more than it did last quarter? What is the level of unemployment? The president is committed to full employment.

WORK AND SPEND

The economy is geared to *work and spend*. The United States has one of the lowest savings rates in the world. Why? Consumer advertising constantly bombards us with one message—buy this and buy it now. The number of advertising impressions oriented to spending money far outweighs the number encouraging us to save it. In fact, most commercials for banks and savings and loans tell us why to choose their institution, not why to save. It's a wonder people save anything. Planned obsolescence of automobiles, fashionable clothing, audio and video electronics, etc. keep the need to spend (and earn) ever growing.

YOU CAN BUY TIME

The work-and-spend cycle may help keep the economy going, but it may not be the best lifestyle pattern for everyone. It is easy to get caught in this upward spiral. It often seems that no matter how much more you make, it's not enough. Your lifestyle catches up—a bigger house, fancier car, more elegant restaurants—where does it all lead?

But here is an alternative plan, and this book advocates it. In the work-and-spend cycle, we never have enough time to do life's basic chores, to relax, or to indulge in hobbies or interests. We are told to stop and smell the roses, but *when?*

Surveys reveal that stress is the number one problem of hardworking adults; it's no wonder in a work-and-spend world where you cannot win. There is always someone richer. There is always something new to buy. There is always some higher rung on the corporate ladder or some larger scale for the growth of your company. *The alternative advocated here is not to drop out but to work, save, and buy time and freedom.* If the word "retirement" scares you, forget it. What you can achieve is the financial freedom to do what you want, when you want, and at the pace you want. These are what the work-and-spend person can never get—the choice of what to do with his day and the luxury of the time to do it.

People are not born to work. Workaholic is a pejorative term. Type A personalities do not have a good prognosis for their lifespan. Yet, many readers of this book probably fit this description. But you can change and by age 55 or younger you may be ready to. Remember what you did through age five: You played and you loved it. The only work you had to do was clean your room, brush your teeth, and so on. And from age 5 until 21 you were probably a student. Sure high school and college takes some work to learn, but there was a lot of time for dates, parties, sports, and the other fun things of life. People are not born to work. It is not instinctive. We learn it. And, because you learn how to work and spend, you can unlearn it. You can learn how to balance work and play when you have the time and no financial pressure. Early retirement is like anything else that you can purchase. You probably won't have as much discretionary income while you're saving or when you retire, but you will have the time to enjoy what you do have.

WORK BECAUSE YOU WANT TO

Remember also, that people who retire early do not necessarily quit working. In recent years, corporate restructurings have provided many workers with early-retirement packages. In many cases when large employers such as AT&T and IBM gave the early-retirement option hoping to encourage a few thousand to leave early, many more than expected took them up on it. Interviews with these early retirees revealed that *they had other plans*. Some wanted to move to a new location, others said they wanted to travel, some said they had wanted to start their own businesses, and this was the time to do it. A survey among retirees in one of the largest pension groups in the country (teachers) revealed the same thing. Those who were the most content in their retirement had prepared for it. They had plans for what they were going to do. The happy people were active people, not dropouts, sleep ins, or do-nothings. People retire and they love it.

WHY AREN'T THOSE PEOPLE AT WORK?

If you have a 9 to 5 job or work in an office or plant, try this experiment. Take a day off from work during the middle of the week and plan some activities in town. You will be surprised at how many people are out and about at all hours of the day. You may wonder: What do these people do? Why aren't they at work? Even in town people use their free time to commute during nonpeak hours, shop without the crowds; go to movies, plays, galleries in the midday; do banking; get groceries and gasoline, and many other chores at their leisure.

When time is your own, why take a vacation during the summer months when everyone else does? April, May, September, and October are beautiful months to vacation in the United States. Many retirees have two homes. Two condos in resort areas can be as inexpensive as one house. How about a winter home in Palm Springs and a summer home in Greenwich, Biloxi, or Sun Valley. Choices. That's what you have when you have health, money, and time through early retirement.

I WANT IT ALL NOW—BUT

Probably the reason most people do not plan to retire early is because they do not think it is possible. This book will demonstrate that it is. However, the second reason why people do not plan to retire early is that when you are 25, 30, or even 35, you want to spend it now; you're moving up the ladder and you love the challenge of your work. Accordingly, you cannot visualize the possibility that your career might slow or stop, that you could become bored with your work, or that you could even be demoted or fired. Popular books have documented the stages or passages of life and most young people have heard about the 40s mid-life crisis. But when you are in your 30s, it's very difficult to imagine it or to believe that it can happen to you. Often by the time a person wants the opportunity to change his or her life, it's too late. They are stuck in the work-and-spend cycle, trapped in an unfulfilling job with little prospect for advancement or new rewards. In the 1980s we had the *me* generation that wanted everything now. They got it now. But that means just what it says—having it now, not later. It's a prescription for a lifetime of work and spend, waiting for the company to tell you when you can retire—and the news is usually not good.

THEY DON'T WANT YOU TO RETIRE EARLY

In a study conducted by Hewitt Associates of companies in the United States, 40 percent said that the earliest age a 30-year employee could retire with unreduced benefits is age 65. (See Figure 2–1) Another third of companies said it was at age 62. Only 15 percent of companies allowed retirement with full benefits at age 60, and a measly 7 percent allowed it at age 55. Let's face it, companies do not want you to retire early. The government does not want you to retire early. The IRS will charge you a 10 percent penalty for taking *your* money out of *your* retirement IRA if you do so prior to age 59 ½.

If you want to retire early, *you have to do it yourself,* using the system to your best advantage. Because our institutions dis-

FIGURE 2–1
Time to Retire

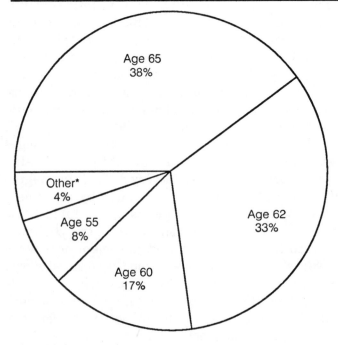

*Age 64, for example

Source: Hewitt Associates

courage early retirement and the culture encourages spending over saving, you have to want it badly or it won't happen. That's why it's important to think about life after work. Imagine it, dream about it, and sample it on your days off from work. Are you doing everything that you've always wanted to do? Would you eventually like to try something new? Would free time allow you to have some experiences that you have missed? Make a list of all the things that you would do if you retired early. If it's a short list, forget about early retirement. If it is a long one, then maybe it's worth working for. If you want to keep working, would you feel more at ease just knowing that you could afford to quit?

WHO ARE YOU WITHOUT YOUR JOB?

Now, the final issue in life after work: who are you without your job, career, title, power, and prestige? Many people fear that they would be no one. In high school we all started at the same place. But in work life, you've broken out of the pack. Maybe you have a lot more now than those high school friends who are selling used cars or having Tupperware parties. But who would you be at the high school reunion when everyone is bragging about their status and you are out of work? There are two answers to this question. Without the job title and trappings you will find out who you really are and you will like it. The second answer is that in this hypothetical competition of the high school reunion, you will find that you have the highest status of all. Everyone will be envious and want to know how you did it. Early retirement can be the ultimate cap to a successful career.

CHAPTER 3

RETIREMENT IN BABY BOOM AMERICA: 2010—2030

If you are in your 30s or 40s you will retire during the first two decades of the 21st century. If you are thinking about early retirement, you need to take a hard look at what corporations and what government offers. What you will find is not encouraging. Even if you hope to retire at 65, the trends are not encouraging. Retirement in 2020 may be much more difficult than it is today—*unless* you plan your own way to achieve it. Although the future is impossible to predict, let's look at some recent trends and draft a scenario of what you might face when you retire between the years 2010–2030.

DON'T COUNT ON THE COMPANY

Company pension plans have improved over the years. Newer types of plans such as 401(k), 403(b), SEP, ESOP, and the traditional defined contribution, defined benefit, and profit sharing plans increase the options to help you save for retirement. The tools will be discussed later. Their use is a must if you are to save smart, but don't assume the company is watching out for you. You have to manage how you will use these tools. One major problem the worker faces is the disloyalty of the employer.

DISLOYALTY OF CORPORATE AMERICA

In our parents' or maybe grandparents' day, a person joined a large corporation and stayed on for life. The worker who received his 35-or even 40-year pin was common. The company took care of its workers with insurance and pensions. Yet anyone working today knows that scenario is obsolete.

Most companies *do* offer a pension plan, but workers often do not stay around long enough to build it sufficiently into a true nest egg. As more baby boomers went to college, they found it was often necessary to move around to enhance their job status, title, and pay. The average persons hired from college or graduate school stay less than three years on their first job. Most pension plans require five to seven years for full vesting. And few young people pay any attention to retirement benefits— that's something to consider about age 50! So, by age 40 many employees have moved three or four times and have little vested pension money.

The problem has become worse. In the mid-80s, leveraged buy-outs, acquisitions, and mergers have lessened job security to the extent that few executive-level employees can hope for a 25-year career.

The college graduate or MBA rarely foresees this pattern until it's too late. Business schools teach how to manage *their* business, but not how to manage *yours*. If employees had a clearer vision of the future they would recognize that their corporate employer is more of a consulting client than a parent.

YOUR CORPORATE EMPLOYER: CLIENT—NOT PARENT

The key difference in this distinction is that a parent always has *your* best interests at heart and thus you never have to think about trust. As a consultant, however, the clients use you only as long as *they* need to. Your pay is a fee for services. You are a private supplier of services with the need to have all the functions of a separate company—production, accounting, finance, pension, and so on. This perspective forces you to maximize your short-term and long-term well-being rather than assume that your client will do it for you. As an independent consultant you *know* you are alone and that only you can assure your future. You must plan your own retirement; no one else will. If throughout your career you plan for *you*, early retirement is feasible.

But many corporate employees continue to think of ABC Corporation as "Daddy." If you shift perspective and *believe* the employer is a client, you will take control of your future by beginning to ask about your retirement options. Many employers do offer options, and you need to study these. Also, legislation has forced employers to offer minimum vesting schedules: (1) either no vesting for 5 years, then 100 percent or (2) 20 percent after 3 years; 40 percent after 4; 60 percent after 5; 80 percent after 6, and 100 percent after 7. Remember, you get all of the money you put in, but maybe none of theirs if you leave too early. It's not uncommon for employees to leave (e.g., after four-and-one-half years) with nothing from the employer when they would have received all five years of employer contributions six months later at the five-year anniversary.

THE FIFTEEN-YEAR CAREER

Another observation about corporate jobs is that most people have no more than a 15-year career. That is, after working from age 25 to 40, their career status is set. If they have reached a high-level executive status, they may advance further. If they are still at a middle-level or lower-level rank, they are probably stuck at best. Managers above age 40 find further promotion difficult to achieve and, in some cases, such career stagnation can be a prelude to termination. To make room for the new blood, the young turks, companies are forced to move out the middle manager. These trends are further reasons why the smart worker should begin to build his financial freedom at an early age. Building a retirement base at 40 plus is tough when your career has stalled or you are out of work.

FORCED EARLY RETIREMENT

The patterns of planned retirement have changed over the years. Young workers often say they never intend to retire. However, this attitude changes for a number of reasons. Once past age 40, the excitement of the job often wanes, and it becomes clear to the individual that they will not become president of the firm, or whatever their ultimate goal. Even those who achieve that goal begin to ask themselves, "Is this all there is? Now what?" The result is that viewpoints toward retirement change. In a national survey of 897 executives, most said they planned to retire prior to reaching age 65. Their post-retirement plans included paid employment, volunteer work, teaching, and special interests.

But sometimes this early retirement is "forced" by early retirement packages. The following headlines began to appear in newspapers during the late 80s:

- Pacific Telesis Offers Early Retirements
- Indiana National Corporation To Offer An Early Retirement Program to Eligible Employees In Efforts To Control Expense
- 6200 Exxon Employees Accept Offer Of Early Retirement
- Firestone Will Offer Early Retirement Plan To 1000 Employees
- Phillips Petroleum Company Encourages Early Retirement of Employees In Restructuring Effort
- Early Retirement Plan Surprise Hit At DuPont
- At Eastman Kodak: After 35 Years Employees Could Receive Full Benefits Upon Retiring As Early As Age 55
- Montgomery Ward Studies An Early Retirement Plan
- Mellon Is Offering Early Retirement To 300 At Bank
- Early Retirement Plan Offered To 2000 At CBS
- International Paper Offers 1000 In United States Early Retirement
- Norfolk Southern Offers Early Retirement To Trainmen and Switchmen

The trend toward downsizing of companies occurred for a variety of reasons—including cost and profit pressure, foreign competition, mergers and acquisitions, takeover threats, advancing technology, and just the glut of baby-boom middle management. In a survey of 529 companies by Hewitt Associates, over one-third of companies reported offering voluntary sepa-

ration plans consisting of early-retirement window arrangements and/or cash. In this study, an average of 36 percent of the
eligible employees accepted the early-retirement option.

The "options" to retire early are great *if* you can afford to
exercise them. The only way that can happen is if you have
independent retirement savings. The average private pension
today is just over $6,800 a year! This is not a scare tactic; it's a
fact. Retirement benefits are no different from salary, health
insurance, or any other perk. Study what your employer offers
and predict your own future income from what you learn. You
may be surprised. You can't count on the company and, unfortunately, you can't count on the government.

DON'T COUNT ON THE GOVERNMENT

A public debate has ensued about the anticipated retirement
problems of the first 50 years of the 21st century. In a nutshell,
the problem is that at present there are approximately 3.3 workers for every retiree. By 2020, there will be less than two workers
for each retiree because the large number of baby boomers will
retire, while the labor force will grow at a much slower rate.

Two related concerns have been raised. The large number
of very elderly people will place an economic strain on the entire
economy. In his book, *Born To Pay,* Philip Longman raises the
issue of how we, as a society, will decide the amount to spend
on health care. "At some level of expenditures for health care,
particularly if they go largely for patients who have little prospect of returning to productive labor, come at the expense of
future economic growth."[1] In 1987, 11 percent of the GNP went
to health care. This is about the same as the percentage of the
population over 65. What will happen in 2030 when the percentage goes to 22 percent over age 65?

In a 1987 American Medical Association survey of U.S. vot-
ers more than half said that they believe Medicare will not be
able to meet the needs of the elderly in the next 15 to 20 years.

---

[1]"Easing the Burdens of an Aging America," *Wall Street Journal,* Section I, September 28,
1987, p. 1.

At present, Medicare annually provides $100 billion in medical care for 31 million elderly and disabled people. Congressional leaders have acknowledged that Medicare is headed for insolvency late in this century or early in the next century unless it is radically restructured. Will our children permit their taxes to increase 30 percent or more to pay for our medical bills?

Not only are there concerns about the political confrontation of the young and the old regarding health care and other issues of the aged, but Social Security will be the major economic problem of baby-boom retirees.

SOCIAL SECURITY IN 2020

It is not a pretty picture. In 2020, the best estimates predict that every one hundred workers will be supporting themselves, their children, and fifty retirees. There is also concern that the mix of workers may affect this outcome as well. Based on current trends, more than 25 percent of these workers will be Hispanic, Black, and Asian. Will these groups be willing to support a largely Caucasian retirement group?

Michael J. Boskin in his book, *Too Many Promises,* says "Public retirement policies in the United States are in deep trouble, and we are heading toward a crisis of unprecedented proportion. The potential economic, political, and social disruption this crisis may cause can hardly be overestimated. The financial planning of millions of citizens, intended to ensure a secure retirement, will be seriously impaired—perhaps completely undermined. Such enormous additional taxes may be required that the economy will be drained of resources badly needed for investment and innovation. Older and younger Americans will be pitted against each other in a battle over public funds. All this lies ahead despite the 1983 Social Security Rescue Plan, which only partially resolved the system's financial difficulties."[2]

---

[2]Michael J. Boskin, *Too Many Promises* (Homewood, Ill.: Dow Jones-Irwin, 1986), p. 2.

This dire prediction is brought home when the economics of social security is examined. Some people believe that as workers we contribute to a fund which earns interest and pays us back at retirement. Nothing like this occurs. Current taxes pay the benefits of current Social Security recipients. In fact, today's retiree would receive no more than four years of benefits with his employer's contribution plus interest! Thus, Social Security is largely a welfare system transferring income from the worker to the retiree. At present, Social Security tax rates are high at over 14 percent with three workers for every retiree. When there are 2 workers for every retiree in 2020, social security tax rates would have to be about 35 percent! Because of the anticipated pressures on the system in the future, a variety of changes are underway or have been proposed.

Prior to 1984, Social Security payments were exempt from income taxes. After 1984, up to one-half of the benefits could be taxed depending on the level of other income. The taxable amount is the lesser of one half of the Social Security payment or one half of income over $32,000 for married couples and over $25,000 for individuals. Municipal bond interest must be counted in this calculation. Thus, if your pension, taxable and non-taxable income total, plus one-half Social Security payment exceeds these amounts, Social Security becomes taxable income. Today only 10 percent of retirees pay any taxes on part of their Social Security. It is estimated, however, that 50 percent of retirees who are baby boomers will have some of their benefits taxed away. In the future, lowering these minimums could be a way to help bail out the system by making more Social Security money flow back to the treasury.

Another change in progress is the lengthening of *the normal retirement age*. At present it is 65. *By the year 2000, it will increase to age 67,* thus those born in 1938 or later will be affected. Most predict that it will eventually go to age 70.

Today, a person who retires early at age 62 to 64 still receives a sizable portion of the full benefit. For example, if they retired at 62, they would receive 80 percent of what would be the full benefit at 65. Thus, they would draw 20 percent less for the rest of their lives. After the year 2000, early retirees at 62 will receive 30 percent less.

These changes will not be enough to solve the problems created by the baby-boom bulge. A number of suggestions or proposals have been made:

1. Increase the "normal retirement age" to 70.
2. Reduce pension benefits which now reflect 42 percent of final years earnings to 39 percent or less.
3. Reduce income minimums that allow more social security payments to be taxed.
4. Reduce benefits of early retirees by 45 percent from today's 20 percent.
5. Eliminate early-retirement benefits at age 62.
6. Eliminate cost-of-living adjustments (COLAs) which protect retirees from inflation.
7. Introduce a "means test." No Social Security if income is above a certain level.

Based on commonly used assumptions, the program's obligations by the year 2035 would exceed projected revenues by 50 percent. Either benefits will have to be drastically cut or payroll taxes raised to 35 percent of income! In 1965, the maximum payroll tax for Social Security was only $348. In 1988, it was a whopping $6,750. To meet future needs when you retire, workers would have to pay over $10,000 (in today's dollars) of their salary for Social Security.

Any way you look at it, Social Security is bound to change in the future and these changes will offer less to you if you were born in the baby-boom years (1945 to 1964). Compounding the problem is the status of the United States as a debtor nation. In order to provide for retirement, the country must find a way to pay off its indebtedness and become net savers. So far, the public says, "I want it now, and I won't worry about it until later."

If you hope to retire early—or maybe at all before age 70—you must begin now to develop an individual plan to save and invest for this future. Social Security will not be the salvation of the baby boomer. In fact, given recent saving patterns, most of these retirees may be forced to work until age 70.

WHAT WILL IT BE LIKE

No one can predict the future, but some facts and recent trends can help us develop one scenario about it:

- By 2020, about 17 percent of the population will be over age 65. In 2030, 21 percent will be over age 65. (See Figure 3–1)
- Every two workers will have to support one retiree.
- Retirees will be an incredibly powerful voting block in the country.
- Social security benefits will not be available until age 70. People will not be able to afford to stop working until that age unless they have substantial private savings.

FIGURE 3–1
An Aging Nation

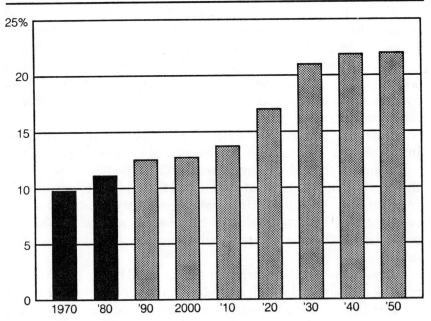

Source: U.S. Census Bureau.

- There will be a shortage of skilled workers so companies will not offer early retirement packages; they will offer incentives to work up to age 70.

A NEW VISION: WORKING RETIREMENT

Stages of work and retirement will no longer be clear cut for older Americans. Even at age 65 and beyond, many people will still be working in new arrangements such as phased retirement, employee consulting, work-at-home assignments, and seasonal on–off work shifts. As much as one third of the over-65 population will be involved in such arrangements.

This vision is motivated by the belief that the average worker who turns 65 in 2020 will not be able to afford retirement. Company disincentives and government Social Security changes will allow only the well off or those who have carefully planned for their later years to stop working.

Even in recent times, the United States government has been altering its policy and encouraging workers to *work longer*. In 1988, federal legislation went into effect forcing employers to continue giving pension credits to workers who continue working past age 65. A decade earlier employers fought a losing battle to prevent a bill which prohibited mandatory retirement before age 70. These employers were concerned that workers would not voluntarily retire at 65, but stay on until 70, creating expensive deadwood and blocking younger workers. This did not occur. More workers retired early after the 1978 law than before it: In 1987 only 11 percent of those over 65 were in the labor force compared to 13 percent in 1977.

In effect, if today's retirees can afford to stop working after 65, most do. Tomorrow's 65-year-old retirees may not be so lucky. If you have planned, saved, and invested for retirement at 55 or younger, here is one piece of good news. Part-time and other employment arrangements can help you supplement your income. Working retirement is an idea that has already caught on with early retirees. A census study in 1987 revealed early retirees are likely to keep working after retirement. Nearly one-third of retirees under 65 sought out another job compared to only seven percent of those over 65 who had retired.

Not surprisingly for working retirees, supplementing their retirement money with wages resulted in higher household income, 50 percent more than nonworkers. They had incomes averaging $3,140 a month or over $37,000 a year! This income consisted of pensions, Social Security, and wages brought in by all members of the family.

Many of these early retirees were still in their 60s. Those who are 55 or younger are even more likely to earn good income from working.

You might allow for supplemental working income when you retire at 55 or younger. If you plan on having outside working income, you may not have to save as much prior to retirement as you would if this saving had to meet all your financial needs.

CHAPTER 4

MANAGE YOUR CAREER FOR GREATER INCOME

Early retirement, financial independence, or whatever you want to call it is the ability to live off your savings and investments so it is unnecessary to work.

Most people are skeptical that they can retire young or achieve this independence until a very old age. For the 99.9 percent of us who do not win the state lottery, get a steep inheritance, or marry a wealthy spouse, our only hope is to plan carefully our working career to maximize our income and develop disciplined saving and investment habits.

Even if you work for someone else, you probably do not recognize how much income you will make during your working years. If you average $30,000 a year from age 20 to age 55, you will make over a million dollars. If you average $50,000 a year, you will gross over 1.7 million. For many people, the income is there, but they lose it to the government in taxes and to creditors in interest payments. Or they just simply spend it. In later chapters we will discuss the tricks for holding onto your money and keeping everyone's hand out of your pocket.

IF YOU CAN'T MAKE IT, YOU CAN'T SAVE IT

It is common sense. If you can make more income, you can retire that much younger and, therefore, that much more quickly. No matter whether you are age 20 or 40, you need a plan for the working years you have remaining. If you do not take control of your career and manage it, you may end up as many others—in a dead-end job, burned-out, and with no options. The focus of managing your career is to increase your value in the economic marketplace.

LOOK AT THE LONG RUN

Most people make a critical mistake in career planning. They do not try to maximize their lifetime income. They may say that they want to get ahead or make more money, but they don't look at their working life to see how that can happen.

Think about this. The difference between a person who makes a lot of money during his working years and one who does not is the disparity in their incomes 20 years out. Most college graduates begin working when they are in their twenties. What do they make? Some new job entrants have a starting salary of $15,000, $20,000, or maybe even $30,000. So what? The differences in starting pay are nothing compared to the *big* dollar differences when they reach age 45 and beyond. One person may make $40,000 and another $150,000 or more. Thus, the key to making a large total amount of money over your working life is the amount you can command when you're older. What's the difference between these two workers?

SUPPLY AND DEMAND

The answer to making the big money lies in the simple law of supply and demand. The labor market follows this law just like other markets. If it sounds too simplistic, consider this premise:

> You can make a large income if you know or have something important that many companies or customers want and are willing to pay for, but few others can provide it as well.

Let's analyze this premise:

- You have to have knowledge, skills, or contacts that someone wants, sees as important, and will pay for.
- If it's just one or a few who will pay, you won't make as much.

- When many companies or customers compete for your services, your income is likely to go up.
- And, if you are one or just a few who can provide this service or object, you can really call the shots.

So what does this tell you about job selection or career planning:

- Evaluate every job to determine what you can learn or learn how to do that other companies or customers will pay for.
- Identify critical needs of employers in your field that *they* think are important where you can become expert.
- Examine your own strengths and weaknesses in selecting an expertise that you can do better than others.
- Make sure that what you are learning is in demand from lots of companies or customers.

In a nutshell, never take a job that does not increase your value and marketability to others.

CAREER MISTAKES

Few people think this way about their careers. They think about the short run. Here are some examples.

Most people simply choose their first job and all future ones because they offered the highest current salary at the time. There is nothing wrong with current income, but ask yourself, "What will I learn from this experience that I can sell to someone else."

Don't fall into the trap of becoming the expert about your company. Some workers know more about the history, the workings, or the people of *this* company. That is valuable to that company, but will it be valuable to another firm? Often not. Thus you have no bargaining power at the time of salary negotiation.

People get taken in by perks and status benefits—the company car, the office with a window. It is great to feel wanted, but if you are wanted by a lot of others outside the firm, you will know your worth inside.

Don't stay too long at one place. The objective is not job hopping; however, you should learn something new and valuable in every five-year period that you can use to move up to a higher income level. If your own company does not recognize it—which, unfortunately, they often don't—move on. Recall the classic case of the 20-year veteran who has advanced in the firm but has nothing to sell outside. We all know such people. They stayed too long and did not make themselves more valuable: Thus, they are dead-ended at age 45 and fired soon after.

The market changes, but some people don't. This is another mistake. What you learned how to do in your first five years on the job may not be in demand ten years later. The world is moving fast, hence the need for changing the product (you) to follow the market. By age 40, you may become technologically obsolete unless you think long term.

The bottom line is always to think two steps ahead when you are in a job. Don't ask yourself if you're learning something— of course you are. Ask "Am I becoming more valuable to other employers as well as to my own employer." Learn something you can sell to someone else.

LEVERAGE WHAT YOU KNOW

It doesn't do much good to develop skills, knowledge, contacts, and the like if you don't capitalize on them. Companies often speak of leveraging their assets. What they mean is to make the assets of the firm "work harder" at earning more return. You have to do the same thing. Here are some examples:

- Engineers learn a technology or process on the job and start their own firm because now they know how to do it better or cheaper.
- Politicians learn how the government works and go to work for government suppliers.
- Business persons learn about an industry, a process, a market, or a product line and become consultants to other firms in the field.

In these cases people are leveraging knowledge, expertise, contacts, and so on. They acquired these assets working for the large firm or the large government and went out to make money with them.

KISS THE OFFICE GOOD-BYE

Can you make a lot of money working for someone else? Well, it's possible, but it is unlikely. Every large company has some very highly paid executives, but the pyramid is steep and the odds of becoming one of them are small. Unless you are now a corporate executive with a high six-figure income, your best bet is eventually to go out on your own.

Studies of millionaires in the United States reveal that most of them are neither corporate executives nor true entrepreneurs. They did not invent anything new or create a new trend. They started a business just like the ones you see every day—fast food outlets, real estate offices, cleaners, car washes, accounting firms. They learned how to do something, and now they are selling it to a lot of people. This is the key. Ten thousand retail customers may each pay you $30 a year or 30 consulting clients may each pay you $10,000 a year, but it is tough to find one employer who will pay you the same $300,000 a year. And, if you can find 1,000 more retail customers or three more consulting clients next year, you will make $30,000 more, but it is tough to get that kind of raise from one employer.

So, if you really want to maximize your lifetime-career income, target your learning toward eventually starting your own company. Your corporate employer buys from such firms every day.

Manage your career for the long run by always learning something to make yourself more and more valuable. Then go out and make it available to everyone.

CAN YOU RETIRE YOUNG WORKING FOR SOMEONE ELSE?

At the heart of managing your own career is the creation of wealth. This is what will allow you to retire young. You can do it working for someone else, but it is much tougher. The self-employed person or the one who "owns" a privately held corporation has some big advantages.

Theoretically, his income ceiling is unlimited. He can make more if he is willing to work a lot harder. Hard work doesn't always translate to a higher salary in a big corporation.

The owner of a company has some perks that the salaried employee cannot obtain. Much day-to-day activity such as driving, eating, and sometimes even sleeping accommodations can legally be a written-off by the business owner. The road to riches is paved, not just by income. The sole proprietor can put away enormous sums tax deferred for his retirement—something most corporate employees cannot do.

And, of course, another prospect is the selling of your business for a large gain.

DON'T GET RICH TOO QUICK

Be cautious about the get-rich-quick schemes. Two well-known authors who wrote how to make millions in real estate with no money in your power went bankrupt. Many younger people are "taken in" by history. Parents or older friends made a fortune in real estate. But they did it in the 70s when inflation helped every property owner to make money. Ask homeowners in Houston how they are doing now. The point is simply that there is no sure thing or one best way for all time. In the 80s tax laws changed, capital gains rates were eliminated, variable rate mortgages became popular, and deflation dominated the decade. In this environment, it was much tougher to make a killing in real estate.

Another area that promises get-rich-quick schemes is the buzzword career: entrepreneur. Few people in the country are really innovators. Sure, Bill Gates dropped out of school, started Microsoft, and became a billionaire in his 30s. Yet there aren't many people like Bill Gates. How many wealthy entrepreneurs do you personally know? People might as well be advised to become movie stars, presidents of large corporations, or U.S. Senators—the odds are the same. Aim high, of course, but be realistic. Why not aim in the direction where *most* successful people make it? Why not play higher odds where the chances of success are more reasonable? Get-rich-quick schemes are always low odds ventures. Take the high road.

Today the odds are better than 1 in 100 of becoming a millionaire, if you do what others have done:

- Work for someone else and learn a business.
- Learn something you can leverage and sell to someone else.
- Eventually start your own business, capitalizing on what you have learned.

Remember, the big money comes in your later working years. Prepare for this time in the early part of your career and don't try to get rich too quickly.

CHAPTER 5

FOUR STEPS TO EARLY RETIREMENT PLANNING

You have decided to *consider* the idea of retiring early. After doing a little homework and conducting some straightforward analyses, you will be able to ballpark a good estimate of how much you will need to save each year. Once you have completed this exercise, you will be able *to seriously consider* the idea of retiring early. Even if you conclude that the task is too difficult, you will be way ahead in having a peek at what your future now holds given current savings, pension money, social security, and so on.

The next four chapters will offer detail in the four steps of early retirement planning:

1. Develop a Scenario of:
   your future retirement lifestyle
   your current lifestyle
   what you would like to do then
2. Calculate Financial Needs for Your Retirement Period
   anticipate lifestyle
   ability to reduce overhead and expenses
   expectation about working
3. Determine What You Have *Now* To Meet These Financial Needs
   social security
   company pension plans
   personal retirement savings
   liquid assets
   full- or part-time working income

4. **Plan How to Close The Gap Between Future Needs and Current Means**
   the three saves
   tools of retirement saving

CHAPTER 6

RETIRE ON LESS AND LIVE BETTER: A RETIREMENT LIFESTYLE SCENARIO

What will your life be like in 2005, 2010, 2020, or whenever you will retire? Estimating how much you will require in annual income is not easy. Besides inflation, other factors make it tough to know exactly what your lifestyle and financial requirements will be. However, you must develop a scenario of that lifestyle so that you can plan for it.

As an exercise, ignore inflation for the moment and assume you will retire next week! You are 55 years old and have 30 years of life expectancy. What will you do? Where will you live? How will you spend your time? Will you work? Will you move to a different residence? The best way to role play this exercise legitimately is to write a page or two on what *changes* you intend to make in your life from the way it is now. Keep in mind you are age 55. This short story of "The Rest of the Life of _____ (Your Name) _____ " can help you flesh out your dreams, current frustrations, and unfulfilled desires. If you decide that you would do nothing different, that's all right; it's your life plan.

To help you develop this life plan, you should consider some issues that other retirees say helped them. Remember also that if you can afford to live on less money, it will be easier to retire early.

You don't want to cheat yourself in later years by squeaking by. On the other hand, if you aim too high, you may never be able to afford to retire.

As a rule of thumb, roughly to maintain your lifestyle, you need between 60 percent and 80 percent of your preretirement income. This may sound like a significant drop, but consider these factors: You are no longer saving for retirement which could have represented 10 to 20 percent of your preretirement income. At age 55, the kids are (hopefully) raised, your home is almost paid off, and you are no longer purchasing the big-ticket items as frequently. On the other hand, health insurance costs are rising, travel costs are expensive, and some of the perks you got from work may now have to be paid for out of your income.

To put some hard numbers on this, consider the spending habits of today's mature market. According to the census bureau, about 51 million people are 55 or older in the United States (30 percent of all adults). People between 55 and 64 make up one half of this group, people 65 to 75 make up one third and those 75 and older make up about one fifth. The median income in 1986 for ages 55 to 64 was $26,800, while the 65-and-older group had $13,000. Spending habits of the 55-to-64 group are consistent with their life-cycle status. Compared to the average family in the United States, they spend less on housing and education (no mortgage, no college-aged kids), but 3 percent more on apparel, 10 percent more for food (eat out more), and 30 percent more for pension programs and insurance. However, if you can afford to retire early at 55, you can save on these pension expenses.

Those who are 65 to 74 have very different spending habits. They spend 17 percent less on food and 41 percent less on apparel than the average family. But they spend more on health care. Those 75 and over spend less on everything except health care (62 percent more than average).

Now all these statistics do tell one important story. Retirees can and do live on less money. How do they do it: other benefits and life simplification.

OTHER BENEFITS

Retirees have Social Security as early as 62 which is tax-free income unless total income is over the minimums (now $32,000 if married, $25,000 if single). They also receive MediCare after age 65. Seniors over 55 qualify for discounts offered by many restaurants and retail and service businesses.

Retirees are generally conservative investors, owning CDs and bonds. There is no federal or state tax on (in-state) municipal bonds and no state tax on United States government treasury bonds.

Also, tax brackets are very low. For example, a married couple filing jointly, having a taxable income of $15,000, pays about $1,500 in federal and state income taxes, so most of their income is spendable.

LIFESTYLE SIMPLIFICATION

Retirees are no different from anyone else. They can live above their means and spend all they make. However, when on a fixed income they cannot overspend today and hope next year's raises will pay off the debt. Hence the need to have enough money *and* to spend it wisely. One key way that retirees live better on less is to simplify their lifestyles and cut overhead and expenses. For some people, cutting expenses is what allows them to retire early. It may take many years to save enough to have retirement earnings equal to those of a full-time job. Yet a simplified lifestyle can make early retirement a reality.

FINDING A NEW HOME

The biggest expense for most people is housing, so this is the first place to look to cut expenses. Studies reveal that most retirees do not move away; they may sell the large home and move into a condo, but they stay in the town where they have lived for some years. A survey of people 50 to 64 by the American Council of Life Insurance found only 14 percent plan to move when they turn 65. Yet, this trend may be changing. As city life becomes more troublesome with crime, traffic, pollution, and added expense, many retirees may seek a different lifestyle. If you retired early to have new experiences, why stay in the old house in the same place? As baby boomers begin to retire, moving may be even more likely since this generation is more mobile than the previous one. Moreover, most of today's corporate professionals have moved around in search of career advancement.

A new type of retirement community is springing up in America. It's called "the retirement compound." These compounds are more commonly known as country clubs! In Palm Springs, California; Naples, Florida; Myrtle Beach, South Carolina; and many other resort areas, large complexes of condos and single-family homes are being built, surrounded by walls and guarded gates. Inside are complete recreational facilities, such as golf courses, tennis courts, racquet ball courts, health spas, swimming pools, and clubhouses and restaurants. These sometimes self-contained communities "feel" safer to a retired person and are often considerably less expensive than the same facilities in a metropolitan area. Although often perceived for the elderly, the average age of most of these country clubs is 55!

One idea that seems to be catching on is to shop for and purchase a retirement residence earlier in life. While working, you have time to investigate various resort properties and purchase one as a second home, getting the tax breaks and appreciation for the years while you use it. After age 55, you can sell your primary residence and receive up to $125,000 of tax-free capital appreciation, which you can use to pay off the retirement home or use for savings.

Complementing the growth of retirement compounds is the new focus on the ideal retirement community. Rand McNally publishes a book, *Places Rated Retirement Guide,* which ranks the hot spots around the country. The criteria used in the book provide clues as to what retirees desire: climate and terrain, low housing costs, money matters (such as tax rates and cost of living), low crime, health care facilities, and leisure and entertainment offerings.

In particular, states and municipalities differ drastically in their tax structures. If you live in New York, Boston, Los Angeles, Chicago, or some other large city, you might be amazed at the small amount of income and real-estate taxes you would pay in certain areas.

Housing costs also differ dramatically. For example, a study of housing costs conducted in 1987 by the ERA revealed that the average home was $158,000 in the East and $136,000 in the West, but only $78,000 in the South and $69,000 in the Middle West. Imagine what you might pay for a wonderful house in Rand McNally's top ten retirement communities:

Murray—Kentucky Lake, KY
Clayton—Clarkesville, GA
Hot Springs—Lake Ouachita, AR
Grand Lake—Lake Tenkiller, OK
Fayetteville, AR
Saint George—Zion, UT
Brownsville—Harlingen, TX
Bloomington—Brown County, IN
San Antonio, TX
Port Angeles—Strait Juan De Fuca, WA

These "towns" may seem a little small and could give you culture shock if you moved to one of them from Manhattan; still recent trends show rural counties in the United States growing faster than the big cities. When you do not have to work in the chaos of a large city, you may not want to live there. You can escape the commuting costs, and you won't have to buy new suits every year or have the big cleaning bill for the office wardrobe. In southern and western areas of the country, heating bills are far lower. Also the cost of entertainment in a smaller town is not as high as in the big cities. Depending on where you live, moving can make a big difference in your expenses.

WHAT TO DO

In drafting your scenario of a retirement lifestyle, be sure to consider what you intend to do with your time. Maybe you would like to teach, consult, or do part-time work.

Imagine a typical day, month, or year. What will you do about exercise, sports, and hobbies? Will you try something totally different from the first two-thirds of your life? Maybe you could go back to school and take courses in a new field? What about a second career? Will you spend time traveling, doing volunteer work, or just relaxing? Early retirement means the chance to do what you want. This is the time to imagine what that will be.

QUANTIFYING THE VISION

After you finish drafting the scenario of your retirement years, think about it a few days and make any revisions or additions that come to mind. Now go back to the exercise started earlier in the chapter: You are gong to begin your early retirement next week. How much money would you need annually to support the lifestyle you envision?

$_____

annual income needed in today's dollars

CHAPTER 7

HOW MUCH DO YOU HAVE IN YOUR POCKET NOW?

You probably already have a few things that can help you move that much faster toward your goal of financial independence and early retirement. It may take a little homework, but answering the following questions will help you to know where you stand now:

- What is the current value of vested benefits in any company pension plan you now have? At current rates of contribution, what annuity (income stream) could be provided if you left the firm at age 55 or younger? Even if the company does not allow early retirement, you may have benefits upon termination that could be rolled over into an IRA.
- What is the current and projected future value of any IRA you or your spouse may have?
- What is the current and projected value of other financial assets or savings such as stocks, bonds, CDs, money market/ savings accounts, etc.?
- What is the net equity in your home? Second home? (Market value less mortgage remaining.)
- What value do you have in other income-producing property? What current and projected income flows?
- What is the cash value of any ordinary/whole life insurance policies you may own? What will be the projected value when you retire?
- Do you have valuable collectibles such as gold, silver, diamonds, rare coins, or stamps that could be liquidated even-

tually? What is the collection worth now and into the
future?
* Do you own a business that has a market value? What is
its value?

A SELF-CONDUCTED FINANCIAL AUDIT

Put the pieces together in a financial statement. Using your self-
conducted financial audit, attempt to answer the question "What
retirement income could I have at my target age for retiring if
I did nothing different?" Maybe by simply doing what you have
been doing—contributing to company pension plans, IRAs, savings accounts, investment portfolios, etc.—you will have the income stream you determined you need to support your retirement lifestyle. If you find that there is a gap between your needs
and current means, then you must find new avenues for saving
to close the gap.

The first step is to determine what monthly income you could
generate from company pensions, IRAs, personal savings, etc.
(see Table 7-1). Then estimate the current and future value of
assets you have that could become income-producing, such as a
sale of real estate. Likewise, estimate what current and future
debts would be. Finally, to help gauge what your cost of living
would be at retirement, determine current living expenses and
estimate which would remain and which would significantly
change at retirement.

Don't worry about allowing for effects of inflation yet. This
will be dealt with in the next chapter.

Examine these financial statements to see how the total
monthly income in the year you retire compares to your projected
living expenses and to the amount you said you would need
(Chapter 6).

* Is there a significant gap?
* Can you close the gap by liquidating or converting assets
to income producers?
* Are there collectibles that you would willingly sell upon
retirement?

TABLE 7–1
Simplified Personal Financial Statement

Income (sources of retirement income)

	Monthly Income Now	Monthly Income in Year You Retire
Company Pension	_____	_____
Profit Sharing	_____	_____
Trust Accounts	_____	_____
IRAs	_____	_____
Personal Financial Portfolio	_____	_____
Social Security	_____	_____
Other	_____	_____

Assets (that are or can become income producing)

	Current Value	Projected Value at Retirement	Monthly Income Potential at Retirement
Primary Residence	___	_____	_____
Second Home	___	_____	_____
Other Real Estate	___	_____	_____
Annuity Contracts	___	_____	_____
Stocks/Mutual Funds	___	_____	_____
Life Insurance			
Cash Values	___	_____	_____
Business You Own	___	_____	_____
Collectibles	___	_____	_____
		TOTAL =	_____

Debts

	Current Amounts	Projected Amount at Retirement
Mortgage	___	_____
Loans	___	_____
Installment Payments	___	_____
Other	___	_____
Future Obligations (such as college education)	___	_____
	TOTAL =	_____

TABLE 7–1—*Continued*

	Living Expenses	
	Current Amounts	*Projected Amount at Retirement*
Food	_____	_____
Housing	_____	_____
Utilities	_____	_____
Taxes	_____	_____
Medical	_____	_____
Insurance	_____	_____
Transportation	_____	_____
Clothing	_____	_____
Education	_____	_____
Travel	_____	_____
Entertainment	_____	_____
Miscellaneous	_____	_____
Retirement Savings	_____	_____
TOTAL =		_____

- Do you have insurance cash values that can be annuitized?
- Do you plan to sell your primary or secondary residence? What could the equity generate in income?
- Would a reverse mortgage be a better way to tap this equity?
- Are there stocks or mutual funds that could be converted to income-producing bonds or annuities?

Is there something you can do now or during the next 10 to 20 years prior to retirement to increase your later income?

- Is there a large enough difference between your current income and expenses to permit you to save more?
- Can you contribute more to an IRA or other personal retirement account?
- Can you alter contributions to your company pension plan to increase the later return?
- Is your savings earning substantial income or are you too conservative?

- Can you pay off consumer loans more quickly to free up cash flow for saving?
- Do you have too many credit purchases necessitating large-interest expenses at high credit card rates?

QUANTIFYING YOUR STATUS

In the last chapter, you quantified a vision for retirement by specifying what income you believed you would need for those years. Now quantify your *present* ability to meet those needs. Given your present retirement plans, savings, income-producing assets, etc., what level of annual income would you be able to generate then (in today's dollars)?

$_____

annual income present status would
provide in today's dollars.

THE GAP

By subtracting the amount you need from what your status now provides, calculate how much of an income annuity you must save for between now and your retirement date.

$_____

annual income gap

UNDERLYING ASSUMPTIONS

The ease and speed with which you can retire depends upon how much money you can earn and how much money your money can earn. Chapter 4 focused on helping you plan to earn more income during your working career years. The other issue—how much return you can expect on your money—is likewise critical.

Some investment counselors, mutual fund managers, and the like claim that they have averaged 15 percent or even 20 percent per year. Obviously, if you could achieve that level of return, your wealth would grow quickly. While claims of 15 to 20 percent returns may be true, they may represent only a partial truth. They may reflect a short-term period of record performance that is not sustainable in the future. And since high returns usually go hand-in-hand with a high risk, those high performers may have subjected investors to tremendous risks to which you would never wish to be exposed. As a general rule, it is unrealistic to base your retirement plan on the assumption of such high returns.

In most of the examples in this book, an inflation-adjusted or *real rate of return* of 5 percent has been assumed. The real rate of return is the actual return less inflation. Looked at historically, this rate has been achieveable over long periods by investors in common stocks and, during the most recent decade, by bondholders. During the period 1926 to 1986, an era that included the Great Depression, a number of recessions and wars, broadly diversified investors in common stocks have experienced a 7 percent compound real rate of return. That performance has been even higher in more recent decades. The real return for corporate bond and U.S. Treasury bonds—lower-risk investments—has been just under 2 percent during that 1926 to 1986 period, but has exceeded 5 percent during the 1980s. Risk-free rates reflected in Treasury bonds have ranged from 8 to 10 percent lately, while inflation has remained in the 4 to 5 percent range.

The underlying thrust of retirement savings plans should be to achieve tax-deferred earnings of 5 percent or more above the rate of inflation using conservative investment vehicles. In order to achieve this rate of return, you may have to take some risk, such as purchasing common stocks and corporate bonds. Many good books are available on this subject, and legions of financial advisors can counsel you. The 5 percent real rate of return as assumed in this book is believed to be a realistic goal.

CHAPTER 8

HOW MUCH WILL YOU NEED IN YOUR POCKET THEN?

This chapter is designed to give you an idea of how much you should save every year to close the gap between future income needs and current means.

FOR THOSE WITH "NUMBER PHOBIA"

Of necessity, some tables and numbers are used; however, for readers who fear anything that looks complicated, be reassured that none of the exercises require anything more than simple multiplication. However, if you would prefer to skip the Early Retirement Planning Worksheet, two simple tables have been devised to suggest a ballpark estimate of how much you will need in savings to retire young. These can be found on pages 56 and 57. If you are willing to do a little multiplication, the worksheet can provide a more precise estimate.

WE WILL ALL BE MILLIONAIRES SOMEDAY

It is true. Saving $5,500 a year at 10 percent interest from age 25 can make you a millionaire at 55. But a million dollars then won't buy what a million dollars will today. In fact, in another 30 years, at 5 percent inflation we may all be millionaires! The average household today having a net worth of $233,000 will find that equal to a million then. Even today one out of every 100 households is a millionaire. To plan your needs in, say, the year 2013, you must know what a dollar will buy then. At 5 percent inflation, it will buy about what 30 cents does now, so you need to save enough for more than three of these dollars to buy what one will today. Here is what inflation can do to dollars you get in the future, (see Table 8–1).

Predicting inflation is difficult. Prior to the 70s and the oil-fired inflation of that period, the United States had a historical inflation rate of 3 percent. Most economists are predicting a 5 percent inflation rate for the foreseeable future. Even this modest rate will mean you will need over $2,500 in 20 years to be worth today's $1,000.

INFLATION CAN HELP

Although those retirees on fixed incomes yell when inflation soars, there are some "benefits" to a pre-retirement saver. Inflation generally increases the value of your assets. During the 70s when housing prices skyrocketed, many workers reported that the appreciation in their homes was greater than any cash they were able to save from their salaries. In effect, homeowners got forced savings that could be valuable, especially if they moved to a smaller home or a cheaper area upon retirement. A related plus is that $125,000 in capital gains from selling your house can be excluded from taxes one time after you reach age 55.

TABLE 8–1
How Much You Would Need N Years from Now at Various Rates of Inflation To Be Equal to $1,000 Today

Rate of Inflation	Value of $1,000 Today	Needed in 10 years	Needed in 20 years	Needed in 30 years
5%	$1,000	$1,629	$2,653	$ 4,322
8%	$1,000	$2,159	$4,661	$10,063
10%	$1,000	$2,594	$6,728	$17,449
12%	$1,000	$3,106	$9,646	$29,960

At the grim rate of 12 percent inflation, thirty years from now it would take almost $30,000 to buy what $1000 could buy now.

Inflation can also help to boost income. If you save some fixed percentage of your income, the dollar value will increase as your salary increases with inflation. Savers such as those working toward early retirement want high real rates of return. When bond interest rates rise in anticipation of inflation as they did in the early 80s, savers are benefited.

INFLATION CAN OVERSTATE

The Consumer Price Index (CPI) that the government computes is the best indication we have regarding the cost of living. For retirees, however, it may overstate. An early retiree should aim to have his residence paid off or at least to have a small fixed mortgage. Thus, inflation in the cost of housing may have little effect on the retiree's budget. When you are retired, you have more time to shop and you can do so more wisely than when under the time pressures of a nine-to-five job. Finally, some revenues such as social security do have cost-of-living escalators that can minimize any damage to purchasing power.

HOW MUCH TO SAVE

This is a complicated issue that is not solved by simple calculations. In Chapter 6, you examined your expected future lifestyle to determine what amount of income you would need. In Chapter 7, you estimated how much future income you could expect to have based on what savings, pensions, and other income-generating assets you have now. Theoretically, you need to save enough to provide an income stream to close any gap between needs and means. But it's not simply a matter of needs.

You must determine what you can *afford* to save. Examine your current income and expenses. What percentage of your income are you now saving in retirement accounts (pension plans, IRAs, etc)? What is the current level of your savings in and out of retirement accounts?

Still, it is possible to calculate how much money you will need at retirement to close the gap and provide the income you desire under various assumptions about inflation and interest rates.

DON'T SAVE MORE THAN YOU NEED

The preceding chapters provided some insights to help you decide how much income you believe you will need during the 25 to 35 years of your retirement. Based on today's life expectancy tables, a man aged 55 will live until age 82 and a woman will live until age 86. These averages could change with medical advances, so it is wise then to be conservative and assume you will live longer than your expectancy.

If you desire to leave a sizable estate to your children, your retirement needs are greater. However, if you believe they will not need your help, then you should think of saving only to secure an income for your retirement years. Most retirees are on a fixed income, which is not bad *if* you have an income large enough to support you 25 years later when you are in your eighties. In effect, if you have a nest egg at retirement and draw a fixed amount for perhaps 20 years, the egg can be less *if* you are willing to draw down the principal and have little savings at your death. For some people, this is a scary proposition and they never want to touch that principal. This can be foolish unless you have a strong reason to leave a bundle to your heirs. In the following example, notice the difference in the nest egg that must be saved if the principal is to remain untouched versus that which is drawn down for the same fixed payment.

Example: How much do you need to save in order to pay yourself $50,000 a year for 25 years if your savings continues to earn 10 percent? If you refuse to invade the principal, $500,000, of course. But if you are willing to use the principal so that your savings go to zero at your death in 25 years, you need to save $454,000. If your life expectancy is 20 years, you could save only $426,000 and $380,000 for a 15-year payout (see Figure 8–1).

Table 8–2 will help you know how much you need to save to pay yourself $1,000 a year at various life expectancies and at various interest rates.

FIGURE 8–1
How Long Should You Plan For?

Life Expectancy in Years

Age Retire	Male	Female	Age Retire	Male	Female
45	35.6	40.2	55	26.8	30.8
46	34.7	39.3	56	25.9	29.9
47	33.8	38.3	57	25.1	29.0
48	32.9	37.4	58	24.3	28.1
49	32.0	36.4	59	23.4	27.2
50	31.1	35.5	60	22.6	26.3
51	30.2	34.5	61	21.8	25.4
52	29.3	33.6	62	21.0	24.6
53	28.5	32.7	63	20.2	23.7
54	27.6	31.8	64	19.4	22.8

Source: *Life Insurance Fact Book*, American Council of Life Insurance. 1983 Individual Annuity Table

TABLE 8–2
How Much You Must Save to Receive $1,000 a Year When the Principal Is Driven to Zero.

Life Expectancy Years to Pay	6%	8%	10%	12%
		Nominal Interest Rate		
10	$ 7,360	$ 6,710	$6,145	$5,660
15	9,712	8,560	7,606	6,811
20	11,470	9,818	8,514	7,469
25	12,783	10,675	9,077	7,843
30	13,765	11,258	9,427	8,055

To use this table:
Step 1: Determine your life expectancy at retirement and what interest rate you can earn on your savings.
Step 2: Multiply the amount (in thousands of dollars) you want to receive each year at retirement by the multiplier in the table.
This will tell you how much you need to save (ignoring inflation).
For example, if you determined in the last chapter that you need $30,000 a year for your lifestyle, if interest rates will be 10 percent over your life expectancy of 20 years, you will need to save a total of $255,420 (30 × $8514).

IT ADDS UP

Table 8–3 reveals the yearly amount necessary to save at various rates of interest between now and when you retire to produce $1,000 in savings.

USING THE EARLY RETIREMENT PLANNING WORKSHEET

The purpose of the worksheet is to help you calculate how much you should save every year to close the gap on the amount you need to retire young.

The worksheet makes three simple calculations:

1. It converts the dollar income from today's dollars into the inflation-adjusted dollars you would need at retirement to preserve purchasing power.

TABLE 8–3
How Much You Would Need to Save Annually to Have $1,000 When You Retire.

Years to Save Before Retirement	Nominal Interest Rate			
	6%	8%	10%	12%
5	177	171	164	157
10	76	69	63	57
15	43	37	32	27
20	27	22	18	14
25	18	14	10	8
30	13	9	6	4

To use this table:

Step 1: Determine how many years you have to save before you retire and the annual rate of interest you can earn on savings.

Step 2: Multiply the number of thousands of dollars you want to save for retirement by the multiplier in the table.

For example, if you want to save $100,000 by the time you retire 20 years from now and can earn a tax-deferred 10 percent, you would need to save $1,800 every year (100 × 18).

2. It calculates the additional savings you must accumulate by the date of your retirement to sufficiently provide the inflation adjusted income you want.
3. It determines what annual amount you must save between now and when you retire to sufficiently accumulate the savings necessary to provide that inflation-adjusted retirement income.

EARLY RETIREMENT PLANNING WORKSHEET

I. Goals and Facts:
  1. How many years away is your planned retirement? _____years
  2. How many years will you live in retirement? (Life expectancy at the age you retire—(see chart on page 52.) _____years
  3. When you retire, how much additional income (in today's dollars) will you need beyond what your current means can provide? (The annual income gap from page 46.) $_____

II. Calculations:
  4. The income you seek as stated in number three is in today's dollars. Given inflation, what income would you have to receive upon retirement to maintain today's purchasing power? $_____
    Calculate this by using Table 8–1, page 49. Use whatever inflation rate you believe will occur (e.g. 5 percent). Multiply the number of thousands of dollars in number three by the multiplier in Table 8–1.
  5. How much additional savings will you need to accumulate by the year you retire in order to provide the level of income you want (number four) over your retirement years (number two)? $_____
    Calculate this by using Table 8–2, Page 52. Multiply the number of thousands of dollars of income you want (your answer to number four by the appropriate multiplier in Table 8–2. Be conservative and assume your money can earn a moderate rate of interest (e.g. 10 percent).
  6. How much must you save every year until you retire to accumulate the amount of additional savings you need in number five? $_____
    Calculate this by using Table 8–3, Page 53. Multiply the number of thousands of dollars of additional savings you will need (in number five) by the appropriate multiplier in Table 8–3. Assume a moderate interest rate e.g. 10 percent.

EXAMPLE USING THE WORKSHEET

Background: You are now age 31 and wish to retire in 20 years. Based on the life-expectancy chart, you can expect to live 30 years in retirement (male). Your lifestyle will require an annual income (in today's dollars) of $25,000 beyond what your present pension and assets can provide.

I. Goals and Facts:
  1. *20 Years to retire*
  2. *30 Years life expectancy after retirement*
  3. *$25,000 income in today's dollars*
II. Calculations:
  4. *$66,325 annual income needed then*
        To receive $25,000 of equivalent purchasing power in 20 years at 5 percent inflation, would require receiving income of $66,325. Using Table 8–1: at 5 percent inflation in 20 years 25 X 2653 = $66,325.
  5. *$625,246 total savings needed*
        At a 10 percent rate of interest, saving a total of $625,246 would allow you to withdraw an income of $66,325 every year for remaining 30 years of your retired life. Using Table 8–2: at 10 percent interest for 30 years 66.325 X 9427 = $625,246.
  6. *$11,250 annual savings over the next 20 years*
        In order to save $625,246 by the time you retire, you would need to save $11,250 at 10 percent interest every year of the 20 years you have until retirement. Using Table 8–3: at 10 percent interest with 20 years to save 625 X 18 = $11,250.

MAKING IT SIMPLER

When attempting to calculate how much to save for those 25 or more retirement years, some people have difficulty with compound interest, inflation, present values, and the like. *You should consult a financial-planning expert to assist you in drafting your savings and retirement plan.*

To help you get a *ballpark* idea of what you might need to save, two special tables have been constructed which, given some basic assumptions, relate how much you save to how much income you can expect. Both tables assume an interest rate of 10 percent and an inflation of 5 percent (5 percent true return). Be advised that neither of these may be true for your future.

Table 8–4 will help you calculate how much you would need to save per year to achieve a $1,000-a-year-retirement income.

WHAT IF I SAVE TEN PERCENT?

Table 8–4 is somewhat unrealistic because few people would save the same dollar amount every year. As in the example in the first chapter, you might save 10 percent of your income, but the dollar amounts would grow over time—assuming your salary kept up with and, therefore, grew by inflation. Here is a simple example. Suppose you make $10,000 salary in the first year of

TABLE 8–4
TO RETIRE WITH $1,000 ANNUAL INCOME*

Years to Go Before Retirement	Need to Save Annually	Capital Needed @10% interest to Pay Equiv. $1,000/yr For 25 Years	Equivalent to $1,000 Today
30	239	39,231	4,322
25	313	30,735	3,386
20	421	24,081	2,653
15	594	18,871	2,079
10	928	14,787	1,629
5	1897	11,582	1,276

Example: To retire with the equivalent of a fixed income of $30,000 at age 55. If you are now 35 and have 20 years to save, you will need to save $722,430 (30 × 24081) which will generate $79,590 a year (30 × 2653) which is equal to $30,000 today. This will require saving $12,630 per year (30 × 421).

*Assumes inflation rate of 5 percent, interest income of 10 percent or true rate of return of 5 percent, life expectancy income payout of 25 years, income tax deferred.

your work and your salary for the next four years grows at 5 percent, the rate of inflation. Each year you save 10 percent of your salary in a tax-advantaged retirement account. This money can earn interest at the rate of 10 percent.

Year	Salary	Save 10% of Salary	Value of Saving in Year 5
1	10,000	1,000	$1,464
2	10,500	1,050	1,398
3	11,025	1,103	1,335
4	11,576	1,158	1,274
5	12,155	1,216	1,216
	Total Savings in year 5 =		$6,687

But inflation has been 5 percent so the value of this savings in today's money is $5,526. How much income can this generate for a 25-year retirement (interest rate 10 percent)? $609 a year.

Thus, after five years at 10 percent interest, 5 percent inflation (5 percent true rate), the retirement income of saving 10 percent of salary every year would equal an income of 6 percent of the original salary. ($609 divided by $10,000). Table 8–5 answers this question for other rates of saving:

"If I save X percent of my salary every year in a tax-deferred account, after __N__ years, what percentage of my salary will I have as income?"

TABLE 8–5
Percentage of Current Income You Will Have at Retirement

# of Years to Retirement	% of Your Income You Have Saved				
	5	10	15	20	25
30%	36%	73%	110%	146%	183%
25%	27%	53%	80%	106%	133%
20%	18%	36%	54%	72%	90%
15%	12%	24%	36%	48%	60%
10%	7%	14%	21%	28%	35%
5%	5%	6%	9%	12%	15%

Assumptions: Current and future rate of interest 10 percent. Inflation 5 percent. (True rate 5 percent). Retirement payout is fixed income for 25 years. Interest income, tax deferred during saving period.

Example: If you have 30 years to retirement, and can save 10 percent of salary a year, at retirement you can have an income stream 73 percent of the value of your working income.

Notice the relationship between the number of years to save and the percentage you can expect. If you have 30 years to go, saving only 10 percent in a tax-deferred account will allow you to have an income that is 73 percent of your working salary (this example was illustrated in Chapter 1). But what if you are age 35 and have only 20 years to go? You will have to save 20 percent of your income to have the same (72 percent) income stream. If you are age 40 now, you would have to save 30 percent of income a year. Of course, those who are older now, hopefully, have more current assets and thus a smaller gap between retirement needs and current means.

CHAPTER 9

SAVE EARLY, SAVE MORE, SAVE SMART

How often have you heard people say, "I could retire if . . . ." These "ifs" involve things such as winning the state lottery, picking a stock that went up tenfold, owning a small company that was bought for 50 times the earnings, getting the multimillion dollar inheritance, or breaking the house in Las Vegas. Sure we have all read about these lucky people who have these things happen to them, and we say it won't happen to us. And we are probably right! Yet, thousands of people retire every year and that is *not* the way they do it.

In the United States people are able to retire because year after year they save small amounts that they or their pension fund invests conservatively. Finally it adds up to a lot of money. This is the way to retire at age 65, and it is the same way to retire at age 55 or any other year. Take the high road. The key to early retirement is nothing magical. It involves *The Three Saves:*

Save Early
Save More
Save Smart

WHEN YOUR MONEY WORKS FOR YOU, YOU DON'T HAVE TO WORK FOR YOUR MONEY

The vast majority of retirees achieve their goal by saving and compounding interest. This is one of the most basic tools available to the early-retirement candidate. If you save $5,000 a year for 20 years, without interest you would end up with $100,000. If your money can earn a tax-free 10 percent, you would have an additional $186,000 in interest. At this same 10 percent, your money can pay you a salary of almost $32,000 a year for a 25-year retirement period.

In fact, as shown earlier, almost anyone can become a millionaire if they save regularly and invest wisely. At 10 percent interest, you need put away only $2,259 for 40 years to achieve this goal. If you have 30 years to go, you must put away $6,079. If you have 20 years until you reach your early-retirement goal, you must save $17,460 a year. This again reinforces the value of starting early.

SAVE EARLY

It is common sense that the earlier you start saving, the less you have to save later in your working life. This is because you have a greater number of years to save and your savings earn money so that you don't have to. For example, Table 9–1 shows the power of an IRA for a two-income couple. If they start early and put away $4,000 combined annual contribution, they will eventually have a bundle.

Note that the couple who begins saving at age 25 and earns 12 percent on their money has a whopping 81 percent more at age 55 than the couple who begins saving just five years later. *The penalty for beginning at a late date is enormous.*

TABLE 9–1
IRA Household Contributes $4,000 Annually
Value at Age 55

Started at Age	8%	10%	12%
25	$489,380	$723,772	$1,081,168
30	315,816	432,724	597,332
35	197,688	252,008	322,792
40	117,296	139,796	167,012
45	62,580	70,124	78,616
50	25,340	26,860	28,460

The couple who started their program at age 40 puts a total of $60,000 into their account over the years (15 X $4,000). The couple who began at age 25 put in twice as much (30 years X $4,000), but their retirement fund at age 55 is four to six times larger! If you are past your 25th birthday and you did not start early, there is nothing you can do. But do not procrastinate. Start now or it will be that much tougher next year. One thing you can do is to buy a copy of this book for your children or grandchildren and tell them to start early!

SAVE MORE

In the previous section, you determined how much you should save given your needs, current assets, and saving ability. If you can save more at any given point, do so. Life has its windfalls; sometimes it is a raise, a bonus, a gift, tax refund, inheritance, or just a few extra bucks you have above your planned expenses. You saw what an IRA contribution of $2,000 each year can do. If you could save $3,000 a year—just $1,000 more—you would have a nest egg 50 percent larger at retirement and thus a retirement income 50 percent larger. Even though present law prohibits putting more than $2,000 per person or $4,000 a year per couple in an IRA, there are other ways to shelter the interest income from taxes. More on that will be discussed later.

SAVE WITH A CARROT

One of the most difficult things to do for some people is to *save*. Although we have been criticized as a country of big spenders, our low savings rate is partially due to the age of the baby boom in the high-cost family formation years. As this group shifts its focus to retirement, savings will go up. But forget the averages or trends, what about *you?*

Most people don't save because they do not *really* want to save. For people in their 30s, saving for some far-off, fuzzy future is a low priority. If you had an additional $5,000 this year would you put a down payment on a new car, buy a new wardrobe, take a European trip, or put it in the bank? Of course, there are honest competing demands such as today's living expenses or saving for college. Still, wanting the carrot of early retirement must be near the top of your list for it to happen. Interviews with early retirees revealed that they craved early retirement. They wanted it, planned it, and eagerly worked to make it happen. Some hated their work, had a mid-life crisis, wanted to leave the rat race, or start a new business. Others just wanted the flexibility and options of financial independence. The point is that each had a strong reason which kept them working for this all-consuming goal. You also will not achieve it without this level of incentive.

CREDIT RICH, SAVING POOR

Why are Americans such poor savers? As noted in an early chapter, our culture promotes spending. Owning the bigger and better car, boat, home, etc. is the sign of success. Who ever sees your bank account? Advertising promotes spending, not saving. Planned obsolescence promotes even more spending. But one aspect of the American financial environment differentiates us from most other countries and contributes to the lack of saving: Credit.

According to Gerald Krefetz, in his book *All About Saving,* personal savings as a percentage of disposable income in the United States was at 2.9 percent in 1985 compared to 8.6 percent in 1976.

> "One of the reasons that Americans appear to save less than others is because the United States has made it extremely easy for the average citizen to spend and subsequently take on debt ... Taking on debt, whether it be governmental, corporate, or personal, is now as American as apple pie ... At the beginning of 1986, roughly 19 percent of after tax income was used by consumers to cover their installment debts—a record-high percentage. Indeed the rise in spending in the last few years has been faster than the rise in income. People are going into debt to support their standard of living, or rather, their elevated standard of living. Personal debt amounts to about one third of personal financial assets."[1]

---

[1]Gerald Krefetz, *All About Saving* (New York: John Wiley & Sons, 1987), pp. 40–41.

Certainly the government has not set a good example. Its enormous deficits reflect a point of view that average individuals seem to adopt for their own budgets. But financial institutions are no better. They promote consumer credit, and people willingly pay the 18 to 20 percent interest. Horror stories abound of people who have 13 credit cards and run up a total debt far in excess of their ability to repay.

Credit has become such an integrated system of the economy that it is difficult to function without credit cards. If you have no credit card, you have great difficulty in cashing a check, renting a car, buying theater tickets, and so on. One individual forced to give up his cards said he felt like a "non-person," a second-class citizen.

Credit card use has grown enormously. In 1986, there were 291 million credit cards in use worldwide with credit spending at $224 billion and almost $5 billion in delinquent accounts. By 1990, it is projected that there will be 391 million cards, $453 billion in credit, and $8 billion delinquent. In the United States, the number of credit cards issued from 1980 to 1986 grew 49 percent. Spending increased 125 percent and total debt increased 80 percent.

For the preretirement saver, credit can be the addictive drug that jeopardizes all hopes of early retirement. Day-to-day life is terribly inconvenient without credit cards. You need not give up such cards unless you have no discipline for curtailing growing credit balances. Clearly, when finance charges, revolving charge payments, and installment debt represent twenty- to thirty-five percent or more of your after-tax income, it is impossible to save a sizable percentage of that income.

Thus, an important precursor to structuring an early retirement savings plan is to take control of your use of credit.

SAVE SMART

Much of the remaining chapters of this book deal with the specifics of saving smart. In general terms, what are these ways? When possible:

1. let Uncle Sam contribute to your savings in tax-favored retirement plans;

2. save in tax-free accounts where interest can compound without dilution by taxes;
3. let your employer contribute as much as possible to your retirement;
4. buy appreciating assets rather than depreciating ones;
5. seek advice about retirement planning, saving, and investing;
6. actively manage your retirement investment
7. be conservative—don't try to get rich too quick.

Let Uncle Sam Save For You

Why do it yourself when the government wants to contribute to your retirement? A variety of retirement plans such as IRAs, 401(k)s, and Keoghs have been developed which provide two key benefits to the prospective retiree. They allow you to deduct your contribution from your taxable income, and the future interest compounds tax-free.

Even if you are in a low tax bracket, your taxes will be less if you contribute to a personal retirement fund. Although tax rates fluctuate with the whims of Congress, the top brackets take about 28 percent for Uncle Sam. This means for every dollar you put into your retirement account, the government could be paying you back 28 cents.

After the passage of the 1986 Tax Code, very few tax shelters remained available to the average citizen. Retirement savings is a big one.

SHELTER INTEREST FROM TAXES

After the 1986 Tax Code altered the amounts that individuals could contribute to IRAs deductible from taxes, many people stopped contributing at all. This is shortsighted. Even if you must place after-tax money into such an account, the interest still grows tax-free until you draw out the funds. This principle of tax-free compounding is an incredible advantage in saving.

Fidelity Investments in Boston developed a simple example to demonstrate the point: A person opens two accounts. One is an IRA and the other an ordinary savings account. He contributes $2,000 a year into each one for 30 years at a constant 8 percent interest rate. He pays taxes at an average rate of 25 percent. All monies are left in the accounts, except withdrawals from the savings account to pay taxes. At the end of 20 years, the savings account is worth $60,051, but the IRA is worth $102,477. Results are even more dramatic at the end of 30 years. The IRA is $259,291, while the taxed savings account is worth only $131,072.

Now it is true that the money in your savings account is after-tax money. That is, you can use it in any way you like without further taxes. In contrast, any money withdrawn from your IRA is considered a distribution and is subject to ordinary income taxes. If at your retirement you begin to withdraw the interest on both accounts, then there is a dramatic difference. The IRA could produce an annual interest income (at 8 percent) of $20,743 compared to the paltry $10,486 from the savings account. And both are taxable income.

Another way to shelter interest from taxes, outside a retirement account, is with municipal bonds. Depending on your tax bracket, and the spread between taxable and tax-free bond yields, this could be a smart way to save. For example, if you are in a tax bracket that results in an average tax of say 25 percent, you might get more by saving municipals yielding 8 percent versus taxables at 10 percent interest. Check with your financial advisor.

LET YOUR EMPLOYER CONTRIBUTE

Employee pensions have now grown to where over half of all private-sector employees have some form of pension, profit sharing, or other type of retirement plan. Some shaky plans and a few big ones have had to be rescued by the Pension Benefit Guaranty Corporation. Still, corporate pension plans will be a significant factor in future retirement income. Some plans are optional or require employee contributions, yet if your employer offers to supplement your retirement, why say no?

YOU CAN HAVE IT NOW AND LATER

"You cannot spend all your money during the working years and hope to have very much for retirement." This is not totally true. *Sometimes you can spend it now and have it later!*

All things you buy are not alike. Some intangibles such as travel have psychological benefits, but not financial ones. In other words, after it's over, your money is gone. Some tangibles have value, but they begin to depreciate immediately—such as new cars, furniture, or clothing. Some assets (such as a house) resemble investments and often, though not always, appreciate in value. Even certain hobby items such as collectibles have the potential of holding their value or better. In effect, there are several ways to spend and save or even earn at the same time.

No one would want to orient his or her life around buying for investment. You would miss out on too many experiences that cost money, but have no residual monetary value. Likewise, when you need a new car you cannot search for an investment-grade Packard that will appreciate; however, an awareness of this concept can make a difference in long-term saving. If almost all of your spending during the working years is for intangibles or depreciating assets, you will have to save that much more in financial assets, such as CDs, stocks, and bonds. On the other hand, if you invest in potentially appreciating assets you can enjoy these when you buy them, while letting them form a savings and investment account for you at the same time. The key is to have a *balance* between the four forms of purchases.

Here is an exercise to give you a perspective on how you are doing. Take your checkbook stub for the past six months to a year and roughly classify your spending into these four categories:

1. **Intangibles** (rent, utilities, food, travel)—expenditures where you do not purchase an object
2. **Depreciating Hard Assets** (furniture, clothes, automobiles, sporting equipment, etc.)—expenditures for objects that go down in value from the price you pay for them
3. **Appreciating Hard Assets** (real estate, collectibles)—expenditures for objects that have a potential to hold or go up in value above the purchase price

4. **Financial Assets** (savings accounts of cash, CDs, stocks, bonds, etc.)—expenditures for soft assets that have a potential to hold or go up in value above the purchase price.

In particular, examine the percentage of your dollar outflow to appreciating hard assets. If it is negligible, you may be able to increase your total savings by altering the mix. If your goal is to save 15 percent of your gross income, you may be able to accomplish this more easily shifting some money you now spend on intangibles or depreciating assets to those that appreciate.

Annual Spending Worksheet

	Dollar Amounts Spent Over Time	% of Total	Goal

1. Intangibles
    rent
    utilities
    food
    insurance
    travel
    repairs & other
    services			

Total	$		

2. Depreciating Hard Assets
    automobiles
    furniture
    clothing
    sporting equipment
    books/magazines			

Total	$		

3. Appreciating Hard Assets
    primary residence
    second home
    collectibles			

Total	$		

4. Financial Assets
    saving accounts
    stocks/bonds/CDs
    retirement funds
    (IRAs, etc.)			

Total	$		

Few tax shelters remain under recent tax law changes. Primary and secondary residences is one of them. Inflation can help you save here also. If a first or second home purchase appreciates as much as the cost of funds minus taxes, it can be a good investment. Some financial "experts" advise clients that home ownership may not be a good investment at high interest rates. This is technically true.

For example, you would be better to invest in 8 percent tax-free municipals than to buy a second home with an 80 percent fixed mortgage of 11 percent, an average tax rate of 35 percent and home appreciation of 6 percent:

Alternative 1		*Alternative 2*
Buy a second home		Buy Municipal bonds
Cost =	$100,000	$20,000 capital available
Down Payment =	20,000	
Financed =	80,000	
@ 11% interest	$8,800	earns 8% = $1,600

Cost/Year

Opportunity cost of down payment (8%)	$1,600	
After-tax cost of Mortgage (35% tax bracket)	5,720	
	$7,320	
Appreciation	$6,000	
Net	−$1,320	+ $1,600

In this simplified example, the financial advisor is technically correct: go for the bonds. But, maybe this is bad advice! It assumes people are otherwise indifferent (except financially) to having a second home or having a municipal bond portfolio. Not only does the home provide other benefits, *the bond may never happen.* After being told not to buy that second home, this household may be just as likely to buy a new car, a new boat, a trip to Asia, or any number of other intangibles or depreciating assets. Viewed from this perspective, the second home is the best investment because at least they save some of their money ($6,000 of the $7,320). The example demonstrates what is true *for many people: Given the option to spend or save, they will spend.* The muni-bond alternative of saving $8,800 a year is fictitious. History proves it. Most people gladly pay $500 to $1,000 or more per month for their mortgage, but they would never save that much if the money were returned to them. For these people, even poor investments such as the second home are reasonable vehicles for saving.

If you are one of the people who are not indifferent between spending and saving, at least try to shift some of your dollars that usually go to intangibles or depreciating assets to potentially appreciating assets that can save for you. Maximize your savings by having a large part of your income in the last two categories of the spending mix.

SAVE TWO POOLS OF MONEY

Some early retirees recommend having two pools of money. One for the intermediate term and one for the long term. When you retire at 65, your life expectancy may be less than 20 years. However, when you retire at age 55 or younger, your money may have to last for 25 to 40 years. Rather than trying to make one source of saving last that long, it is better if possible to have two. For example, you might save after-tax money invested in CDs, bonds, or other income-oriented investments to support you for the first 10 to 15 years. Another pool of funds may be in company pensions, IRAs, or the like which can grow tax-free during this period and then kick in at age 59 ½ to 65 to support you through the remainder of your life. Social Security will also kick in during the latter period as will Medicare.

So don't think of retirement as one long homogeneous period. Divide it into, say, 15-year segments (e.g. 50 to 65 and 65 to 80) and plan your retirement income sources separately to fund each segment.

INVESTING SMART

The proposition of this book is that you can retire early without being lucky or an investment genius. If you had to make a 20 percent real return on your money every year to accomplish this goal, it would be a sham. Instead, you can retire at age 55 or younger with a modest income by saving at rates that are available to anyone. For that reason, this book is not oriented to selecting investments. Many other books are available on that subject.

Because retirement money is long-term money, it can be invested differently than short-term savings. If you are 35 and plan to retire at 55, you can afford the trauma of short-term fluctuations to gain the benefits of long-run capital appreciation.

The best advice is to seek help from an expert who can tell you the options and recommend what is best for your portfolio and your proclivity for risk.

SEEK ADVICE AND MANAGE YOUR INVESTMENTS

Inumerable books have been written to provide every type of advice on investments. These can be valuable to help educate you about terms, concepts, and investment ideas. *But,* everyone is different and the best advice can only be given for a specific individual in a specific set of circumstances. Thus, you should seek out professionals to help you draft an early retirement plan that can produce the type of lifestyle you desire. Where do you find such an advisor? Consult the yellow pages of your phone book under "Financial Planners." Some experts are certified financial advisers (CFA). Look also under the heading "Pension and Profit-Sharing Plans" for specialists who can help you analyze your ability to participate in or establish such plans. Other experts such as accountants, insurance agents, and stock brokers can often be of value in planning. In fact, many brokerage houses have a financial planning service geared to the individual. For a modest fee they will analyze your current situation and make recommendations how you might meet future goals such as financial independence/early retirement.

If you have difficulty locating a person you like, contact:

Institute for Certified Financial Planners, 10065 E. Harvard Ave., Suite 320, Denver, CO. 80231; or

International Association for Financial Planning, 2 Converse Parkway, Suite 800, Atlanta, GA 30328; or

National Association of Personal Financial Advisors, P.O. Box 2026, Arlington Heights, IL 60006; or

The Licensed Independent Network of CPA Financial Planners, 404 James Robertson Parkway, Suite 100, Nashville, TN 37219.

Selecting a planner is like picking any service professional. Some may be good for you while others may not. Find one who understands your goals and tolerance for risk. If you are not satisfied with the first one you speak with, interview others until you are comfortable.

A WINNING STRATEGY TO BEAT THE MARKET

Many horror stories abound about the fortunes lost in the stock market. If anyone ever wondered whether the market was like gambling, the tremendous rise of the 80s bull market and the crash of '87 prove that it is. The high rollers may make money, but the little guy usually loses. He buys high when the market is really moving and sells low when he panics after a steep decline. It is hard to make money unless you have time and discipline—just what the prospective early retiree must have in spades.

The strategy that is mathematically proven to beat the market over the long-run is called "dollar-cost averaging." All sophisticated investors know about it, but most are too sophisticated to use it, thus, they rarely outperform the market!

The strategy is simple: You must invest a fixed amount of money at regular time intervals without regard to market prices. For example, you might invest $100 a month or $1,000 at the start of every quarter or $10,000 every January 1st. The amount doesn't matter, but it must be constant and the timing systematic. Notice what this forces you to do. You will buy more shares when the price is low and fewer shares when the price is high. You could buy one stock, a mutual fund, or even treasury bonds—whatever as long as you buy it regularly over a long period of time in the same dollar amounts.

Here is how this averages the cost of purchase. Suppose you bought shares every year for $1,000. In the first year, if a share costs $25, you will purchase 40 shares. In the second year if the stock price falls to, say, $10, you would buy 100 shares, and in the third year if the price goes to $50, you would buy 20 shares. So you now own 40 plus 100 plus 20 shares or 160 shares. In these three years, the average price per share was $28.33 ($25 + $10 + $50/3). But because you bought more at the lower prices and less at the higher ones, your average cost was only $18.75 ($3,000/160 shares). Using this strategy over time, you can see that you accumulate shares at an average price below and therefore better than the average stock, mutual fund, or bonds being purchased. In fact, the more volatile the market, the more dollar-cost averaging works to lower your average cost of accumulation over time. It takes guts and staying power to keep buying the same dollar amount even when your stock, fund, or bond has plummeted!

The conservative way to invest is to diversify in a mutual fund of stocks or bonds using this strategy. If you are young and saving for a retirement maybe 25 to 30 years away, this method can work for you. Remember, you don't pay taxes on capital gains until you sell.

Note, you might think you can do better by just buying lots of stocks when the market is low and selling it when it is high. It sounds easy, but who knows what is high or low? Studies of so-called market timers have proven conclusively that none of the experts has been able accurately and consistently to call the swings in the market. Thus, you are safer with the proven way to beat the market—dollar-cost averaging.

CHAPTER 10

THE TOOLS OF EARLY RETIREMENT

If you want to retire early, you have to "use the system" by taking advantage of every tool that employers and the government offer to help you save smart. These include such things as IRAs, KEOGHS, 401(k)s, and the like. This book is not intended to be an encyclopedia of retirement savings plans, nor does it offer detail sufficiently to make you an expert on this subject. It is intended to show you a range of options to demonstrate how these tools can help you achieve your desire to *retire young*.

IRA: THE DO IT YOURSELF PENSION

Congressman Eugene Keogh is declared to be the father of the Individual Retirement Account (IRA). In 1962, his bill was passed to give unincorporated, self-employed people the ability to create their own retirement plans. These "Keogh Plans" still exist. However, because many employees had no pension even through corporations, the Economic Recovery Act (ERISA) was passed in 1974 and created IRAs. At that time they were limited to people who had no pension plan. In 1982, they became available to everyone. In 1987, they again became restricted. If you are covered by a company pension plan, you *may* not be able to have a fully deductible IRA.

IRAs offer two key benefits to those eligible: tax-deductible contributions and tax-free earnings. As noted in previous chapters, this helps the saver by having Uncle Sam contribute to your account which significantly increases the power of interest compounding since nothing is taxed until you are ready to withdraw the funds at retirement.

Since the limits of an IRA are $2,000 a person ($4,000 a couple), it is not a way to shelter a large percentage of income for the high-income worker. Nevertheless, every bit helps and IRAs should be seriously considered by everyone. Since you do not have to put in the maximum allowed in any given year, there is great flexibility for the individual who may or may not be able to afford this level of savings every year. Another small disadvantage of IRAs for some is that there is no deduction possible if you have capital losses. At present, a capital loss from investments can be used to offset up to $3,000 in passive income outside a retirement account. Thus, IRA gains are tax-free, but IRA losses have no value to offset taxes on income.

The IRA is the true do-it-yourself pension because you can invest the money in any way that you see fit, except hard assets such as precious metals, art, antiques, and other collectibles. However, the 1986 tax law does permit owning gold coins issued by the United States Government.

WHO CAN SAVE?

Who can save in an IRA and how much? It keeps changing, but according to the 1986 tax code:

Anyone who is self-employed, or who is not in a qualified pension plan at work can use an IRA without restriction. If this is you, you may contribute up to $2,000 of earned income. A one-income family may contribute up to $2,250. The non-working spouse may not have income above $250 for the family to qualify. If you do have an employer-maintained retirement plan, you may have restrictions. Employer plans include pension, profit sharing, stock bonus, annuity plans, Simplified Employee Pensions (SEP), United States or State government plans, or tax-sheltered annuities. If you do participate in one of these plans, the restrictions are determined by your income. Couples with less than $40,000 in adjusted gross income and single taxpayers with less than $25,000 may deduct all of their contributions to an IRA. You can deduct some if your adjusted gross is $40,000 to $50,000 for a working couple or $25,000 to $35,000 for a single worker. It is complicated so you should consult your tax accountant. Note, however, that everyone can still contribute the maximum amount permissible and have the interest grow tax-free, but their contribution *may* be only partially tax-deductible or not at all.

IRAs may not be the best plan for everyone because the amounts are limited. You may be better off with a different retirement plan to be discussed later in this chapter. These plans may allow you to shelter and save a considerably larger portion of your income.

INVEST IN WHAT?

The alternative investment vehicles that can be used in an IRA are broad based and cover the spectrum of risk. At present only a little over 14 percent of all IRAs are self-directed. The rest are deposits made in commercial banks, savings and loans, credit unions, life insurance companies, and mutual funds. On a self-directed account, a brokerage firm or financial institution sets up an account where you choose and manage the investments. You may choose from money market deposits, CDs, stocks, bonds, mutual funds, Ginnie Maes, and a host of others. Remember, however, that with tax- free interest compounding you may not have to make exceptionally risky investments to make money.

HARVESTING THE IRA EARLY

A critical consideration for the individual seeking early retirement is to have a plan to extract his or her money. This is somewhat complicated because the Internal Revenue Service collects a non-deductible 10 percent penalty for any withdrawals made prior to age 59 ½. You may "roll over" money to another IRA account. But if you hold it more than 60 days, it is treated as a withdrawal and you would be charged the 10 percent penalty plus taxes at your current rate. Also, you may not borrow from these accounts or use them as collateral for a loan. So how do you get your money early?

Remember, the best way to save for retirement is with two pools of money—a savings plan outside of these retirement accounts for the early years of retirement and these accounts for the later years over age 59 ½. However, if you need *some* of this money early, it can be done without penalty. One of the least noticed provisions of the 1986 tax act is a regulation which provides this way to extract funds prior to 59 ½ (other than by disability or death). An IRA owner can withdraw money from his account at any age if the money is withdrawn in substantially equal payments over a period that corresponds to the taxpayer's life expectancy as reflected in IRS tables. In other words you withdraw money as if your IRA were an annuity. If you are quite young when you retire, say early 40s, you may only be able to take 3 to 5 percent of the value of your account each year. The amount you take can grow slightly each year because your life expectancy declines. Once started, you must stick with this payout plan until you reach 59 ½ or 5 years, whichever comes later. If you have paid out for 5 years at the time you reach 59 ½, you may withdraw whatever you want at that time. Thus, this is a way to make partial withdrawals in the early years of your retirement and still grow the account for the later years when you will withdraw the rest. For more details of this provision, see Internal Revenue Code Section 72(t).

TAX-DEFERRED ANNUITIES

Another tool for savers is the tax-deferred annuity. Under recent tax code changes, deferred annuities purchased from insurance companies provide an alternate way to save tax-free until withdrawal. An annuity is an agreement between you and the insurance company whereby you make a one-time payment or series of payments and they agree to pay you a specified amount over a specified time period or for life. Purchased outside of an IRA or other retirement plan, the premiums you pay are not tax-deductible, but the "interest" appreciation builds up tax-free. Thus, you have one advantage of the two that IRAs offer, and you can contract for large amounts.

For example, suppose you want a "guaranteed" (by the insurance company) lifetime payout of $3,000 a month for you and your spouse beginning at age 59 ½. You could purchase this with a one-time fee at, say, age 40 or make payments until you are ready to retire. In fact, you can buy just about any type of payout plan you want. Since these are private offerings of insurance companies, you should shop around for the best value. Also, check Best's Insurance Reports to get a quality rating of the insurance firms.

Annuities provide some certainty about future retirement payments and they can be bought for a lifetime payout or for some shorter defined period such as 20 years. Since these are insurance products, they offer the provision for loans and there is a cash surrender value on deferred annuities that you can collect if you cancel or your beneficiary can collect if you die. Multiple payment plans, which are set up to have you pay in a set amount every month, quarter, or year, do have the benefit of "forced savings" for people who lack discipline to put money away. There are many types of annuities—fixed rate, variable rate, and so on. Get help in picking one that would be best for you. Remember, the principal compounds tax free, and you pay no taxes on your original (after tax) contribution—only on the interest when you begin receiving payments.

SINGLE PREMIUM LIFE INSURANCE

Single premium life insurance is not what it seems. Single premium life insurance is not really bought for life insurance, but instead is a tool to accumulate interest tax free until you surrender (cancel) the policy. When you do surrender it, say at the time you choose to retire young, you pay taxes on the invested amount at your then marginal tax rate, which could be low.

People who benefit from this tool are savers who can buy lump sum amounts of say $2,000 or more and keep it until the money is needed at retirement in 10 to 30 years. The insurance component is small. This is only a plus. Consider this tool as a way to invest every year and have interest income grow tax-deferred.

Here are some of the benefits. You can get a tax-free loan against any interest accumulation or borrow against principal at no more than 3 percent. For early retiree candidates this is an option you do not want to use, but at least the money is available in an emergency. When you surrender the policy after 10 years or more, you get all your principal back plus interest taxable as current income. If you buy many small contracts over time such as two $2,000 contracts every year during your working years, you can surrender them a little at a time when you are retired and, thus, have the policies in force still earning interest. Be careful to note any surrender charges which can be as high as 9 percent if surrendered during the first three-to-five years. For most policies, there is no charge if held at least 10 years. These policies are sold by insurance agents or financial planners. The security of the policy is guaranteed by the insurance company, so be sure you pick a well-established firm. Note that one benefit of SPL policies over annuities is that you liquidate these when you want to. Annuities are payed to you on a predetermined schedule.

The single-premium policy is a good tool to use in the two pools of money strategy. Use SPLs to generate money for the early years prior to 59 ½, after which IRAs and other pension plan funds can be withdrawn.

COMPANY PLANS

If you work for a corporation, you probably have one of the following plans available to you. Some corporations offer more than one type of plan, so it is prudent to study your options. Questions to ask your employer should concern the level of their contribution, your contribution, vesting schedule, normal retirement date, possibility of early retirement, projected payout schedule, and the like. Also do some homework about the health and safety of the plan. Some plans have been terminated or have failed and not all are insured.

You will notice that most plans are geared for retirement at age 59 ½ or later. Thus, you might ask, "How can these be used to retire when you are considerably younger?" There are two answers. Some plans do have provisions for partial withdrawals during earlier years without penalties. The second answer is the use of the two pools of money strategy discussed earlier. These plans are excellent vehicles for saving in the pool you will use in the later years (age 60-plus) of your retirement.

401(K)

The 401(K) is a salary reduction agreement where you, your employer, and Uncle Sam all save for your retirement. These are salary reduction agreements: your salary is reduced by the amount of your contribution and is reflected as a lower taxable income on your W-2. The maximum allowable reduction is $7,000. The employer usually matches your contribution with approximately one dollar for every two of yours.

The plan is administered by a trustee who invests in a stock or bond mutual fund, or you have options. Appreciation and interest income are not taxed. You pay taxes only when you withdraw after age 59/2. Like an IRA, you get a tax shelter and the potential for tax-deferred compounding, but with the higher contribution limit. The bad news may be that your employer doesn't offer such a plan. Even though still relatively rare, more employers are adding these.

All contributions and interest you make are 100 percent vested. Yet employer contributions may not be. In many of the 401(k) plans, employees are given investment options such as a stock mutual fund, a guaranteed investment contract, or a company stock. Some offer bond funds, life insurance, or real estate.

Some plans have loan provisions, and withdrawals without penalty prior to age 59 ½ are possible under conditions of disability or severe financial hardship. These plans are portable in that they can be rolled over into an IRA if you leave the company. After 59 ½, you may take a lump sum with five-year forward averaging or you may withdraw in regular payments.

Check with your employer to determine if your other retirement plans are affected if you participate in a 401(k); some employers reduce their contribution to other offerings if they contribute to a 401(k). Still, the 401(k) is one of the best plans companies offer.

SIMPLIFIED EMPLOYEE PENSIONS

The Simplified Employee Pension or SEP is generally offered by small businesses, and is, in effect, a special type of IRA. The plan permits the small employer to offer a retirement plan without all the paperwork and cost of some others. The maximum permissible contribution is $30,000 made by the employer ($7,000 is tax-deferred). However, in any given year, it is at the discretion of the employer to make any contribution at all. If one employee receives money, all must. However, the participation requirements are specific. If you are 21 or older, have worked there at least three of the past five calendar years, and earn at least $300 in compensation, you must be included.

One limitation for highly paid employees is the restriction on percentage of income that can be contributed. To make certain that lower-paid employees can receive the same benefits as those higher paid, the percentage that can be deferred by the higher-paid employee cannot exceed by more than 125 percent, the average deferral percentage of all other participants. These restrictions make SEPs less than ideal.

Also, the withdrawals cannot be taken as a lump sum using forward averaging.

In general, SEPs are similar to IRAs in their treatment of withdrawal regulations. You are always vested and the total amount may be rolled over to an IRA if you go to another employer.

The SEP is not a perfect early retirement plan, but it does allow a larger contribution than the IRA, and, an employee who has one can maintain an IRA as well.

PENSION PLANS

In addition to the tax-deferred savings plans such as IRAs and salary reduction plans like 401(k)s, the heart of most retirement plans are private pensions. More than half of all full- and part-time civilian employees have such a plan. However, a company may drop a non-union plan whenever it chooses, so there is no guarantee that your pension plan will continue in the future. What is worse, companies routinely skim money from these plans which are "overfunded." The overfunding occurs because of large appreciation due to stock market increases. But in the crash of October 1987, for example, many pension funds lost millions, and it is not at all clear that all of them will be able to support the growing number of retirees. Also, only about 5 percent of private plans have an automatic provision for cost-of-living adjustments. Thus, if inflation became ugly, your real income would decline significantly. This caution suggests that you should plan and save for your retirement—don't assume the company will take care of you. (See Figure 10–1).

DEFINED CONTRIBUTION AND DEFINED BENEFIT PLANS

Defined contribution and defined benefit plans are the two basic types available to most employees. In the defined contribution plan, the employer contributes a set amount to a fund in your behalf (e.g. 8 percent of salary). This fund is invested, and the amount you receive at retirement depends on the investment performance of the fund. In the defined benefit plan, the employer promises to pay you a specific amount during retirement. The employer contributes enough to accomplish this "defined benefit" based on actuarial tables of your life expectancy.

Trustees are placed in charge of defined contribution plans and knowing their future performance can be only a guess. Examine the past appreciation performance of the plan to judge what its value will be when you retire. In the defined benefit plan, it is much easier. Your employer's benefits office can tell you what you can expect if employment history continues until retirement. A typical formula for this type of plan is 2 percent of the last 5 year's pay multiplied by the number of years in the plan. Thus, if you participated for 30 years, you would get 60 percent of your final few years' salary. This is a great supplement to your saving, but not sufficient to sustain you for say 20 or more retirement years. What's worse, with all the job-hopping, few employees stay with one firm for 30 years.

Another way that employers minimize their payout to you is through so-called integrated pensions that promise a fixed benefit which includes Social Security. Thus, if the defined ben-

FIGURE 10–1
America's Retirement Funds

Value of retirement programs, in billions of dollars

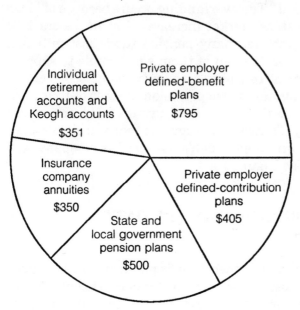

Participants in millions

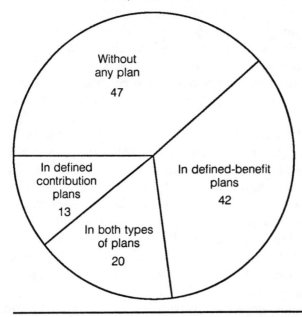

Source: Employee Benefits Research Institute.

efit is $1,000, they will pay the difference between Social Security and this figure. The higher level of Social Security you receive, the less from the company.

In general, normal retirement age for most pension plans is 65 with some allowing a reduced benefit at 62 or younger. These plans are helpful to the early retiree who uses this plan for his later years. A defined contribution plan could produce a lot of money if you start young and invest wisely. A defined benefit plan may be worth less, for if you retire at age 55 with 20 years of service, you might expect something close to 60 percent of your benefit paid when you are 65. (See Figure 10–2) Not great. Probably the greatest problem with these plans for the typical employee who seeks new employment every three to five years is vesting. The employer has the option of zero vesting until five years, then 100 percent or 20 percent after three years, 40 percent after four, and so on with full vesting after seven. The frequent job changer may have no vested pension benefit

FIGURE 10–2
The Effect of Early Retirement on Your Pension Benefits

Age	Average Pay Last Five Years	Years of Service	Typical Pension Benefit Starting at Age 65	Typical Pension Benefit Starting Now
55	$35,000	20	$10,500	$ 6,300
56	37,450	21	11,797	7,550
57	40,072	22	13,224	8,992
58	42,877	23	14,793	10,651
59	45,878	24	16,516	12,552
60	49,089	25	18,408	14,726
61	52,526	26	20,485	17,207
62	56,202	27	22,762	20,031
63	60,137	28	25,258	23,237
64	64,346	29	27,991	26,871
65	68,850	30	30,983	30,983

Assumptions:
1. *Pay increases at 7% for each year you continue working.*
2. *Pension formula is 1.5% of final five-year average pay times years of service.*
3. *Pension is reduced 4% per year for retirees below age 65.*

Source: Hewitt Associates "Early Retirement—Could you pull if off?" *Changing Times,* Feb. 1984, pp. 26–31.

even after 10 years of work, hence the desirability of do-it-your-self and portable plans.

403(B)

If you are an employee of a nonprofit organization such as a school, the 403(b) plan is the government's plan for you. This allows you to make tax-deferred contributions to an insurance company or mutual fund for an annuity. Like the 401(k), the contributions are tax deductible and the earnings are tax deferred so you can take advantage of tax-free compounding. The maximum amount the employee can defer is $9,500, but there are some exceptions. For many people, the 403(b) plan allows you to put away much more money than the IRA. And, an IRA can be funded along with the 403(b) if your salary levels permit.

Withdrawals at early retirement are possible. If you take your withdrawals in the form of an annuity (substantially equal payments over your lifetime), you can receive an income without penalty when you terminate your employment upon retiring.

KEOGH

The Keogh is one of the best tools available for the early retiree. The only limitation is that you have to be self-employed or work for someone who is!

In simple terms, you are probably willing to pay yourself more money in your retirement than is an employer with 3,000 employees. Self-employed people do not have any tools available to them that are not available to companies of any size. It's just that the self-employed are more generous to themselves!

The government created retirement plans for the self-employed because they had no large corporate benefactor to give them a pension. Even now as 401(k)s are limited to a $7,000 maximum contribution, Keogh-defined contribution plans permit a maximum of $30,000. And, if that is not enough, a defined benefit plan under the Keogh provisions permits you to sock away as much as 100 percent of your income! Here is the true reason that entrepreneurs and private professionals can retire early. Like IRAs, these deferrals are tax deductible in the year of contribution and interest earnings compound tax-free. Vesting can be immediate and payout is possible without penalty if you retire early. It should be obvious that being self-employed can significantly aid your progress in retiring at a very young age. Here is how:

Keogh plans are the only remaining retirement plan following the 1986 tax code changes that allow tremendous tax-sheltered savings for retirement. Keogh users are professionals, sole proprietors, independent consultants, contractors, and the like. Many of these people have few if any other employees and that also helps when choosing to save a large proportion of income. You must be an unincorporated business, and own more than 10 percent of the business.

Keogh plans are like IRAs and have many of the same rules, although you can contribute to a Keogh past age 70 ½ (unlike an IRA). In a defined-contribution Keogh, a so-called money purchase plan, you can contribute up to 20 percent of your net self-employment profits or $30,000, whichever is less. Thus, if you have $150,000 or more in profits, you can save $30,000 of it tax deferred. As with other defined-contribution plans, you must contribute a fixed percentage of income every year. This can be raised over time but not lowered. Thus, whether you are profitable or not, you must contribute each year. Another version of the defined-contribution plan is the profit-sharing Keogh. In this scheme you can contribute up to 13 percent of net profits at your option. Thus, in a year when profits are low, you could choose to contribute nothing to the plan. It is also possible to have a plan which is a combination of these two plans. In these defined contribution plans, participating employees must receive a contribution whenever you do and in the same percentage. This can be costly if you have many employees.

The defined-contribution plans are easy to set up. Brokerage firms now offer so-called prototype plans that are somewhat standardized and very inexpensive to implement and maintain. Investments can be self-directed with the same options available as in an IRA. You can have an IRA also if your salary limits permit. What else could you want?

Maybe you want to have tax-deductible savings of even more income. Maybe all of your income. OK, that's the defined-benefit Keogh. As with other defined-benefit plans discussed earlier, you set a target goal of the amount of annual payment you want when retired. The maximum permissible defined benefit is $90,000 at age 65 or 100 percent of compensation for the three highest-paid consecutive years, whichever is less. An alternative is $75,000 at age 55. An actuary then calculates the amount you must contribute annually to have enough savings to fund that defined-benefit income. The IRS permits conservative assumptions about the rate of return you might earn on this savings, thus, large amounts are often necessary to achieve the defined benefit. If you are a little older now, say age 40 and only have 15 years to go, the calculations will require *very* large contributions. You can now see why some people are able to save their entire salary in this type of plan and why it is possible to retire young even if you are older and have a few years to go.

Another benefit of Keoghs is that withdrawals can be taken as lump sum with forward averaging for lower tax impact. Also, they can be rolled over into rollover IRAs. At age 59 ½ or later, you can receive annuity payments of the average of the highest three years of earnings you had up to $90,000 a year.

Even if you have a regular job working for someone else, if you have self-employment income on the side, you can have a Keogh.

Keoghs are not a panacea. IRS rules are stricter than for many other plans, reporting is necessary to the IRS, and of course, you must be able to put this money out of reach since penalties are harsh for early withdrawals. Nevertheless, if you want to retire quickly, start a business where you are the only employee and make a lot of money! This is the plan that can help you put it all away for the future.

MILITARY AND CIVIL SERVICE

Retire early in the military? Anyone in the military knows that they can do it. If you attained regular or reserve status before August 1, 1986, you can retire with 50 percent of final pay at 20 years of service and 75 percent at 30 years. More recent recruits would get 40 percent at 20 years. No private pension plan comes close to this. Civil service workers don't have it as good as the military, but they too can retire at age 55 after 30 years service with more than half final pay. And benefit payments are tied to cost-of-living adjustments (COLAs).

The history of early retirement in the military is a clue for the rest of us. After 20 years when retirement is possible with half of income, many take advantage of it. Think of it another way. If you keep working, you receive only half of your pay since you would receive the other half for quitting and not working! These early retirees usually look for a new second career leveraging the skills, knowledge, or contacts they made while in the service. They can live on half of their salary since the new career may pay as well or better. In a sense, if the new job can pay you more than one-half of your military pay, you will be better off to retire and take the new job. This same logic applies to you even if you're not in the military. Between savings and retirement plans, if you can pay yourself half of your salary at a younger age, say 40 to 55, you might choose to quit and seek a new career leveraging what you have learned in the first one. At least the option to do so is there.

ASK NOW

If you don't know what your pension offers, don't feel bad. A study by the General Accounting Office shows that up to 82 percent of workers in a pension study were wrong about when they qualify for retirement benefits! Half of required plan summaries for employees are faulty, a Labor Department review found. Don't wait to hear from your employer—take the questionnaire on the next page and go ask some questions to get the full scoop on your future.

QUESTIONS TO ASK YOUR EMPLOYER
ABOUT YOUR PENSION

1. What type of pension do you have?
   Defined benefit
   Defined contribution
2. Is the plan integrated with Social Security?
3. Does the company offer a 401(k)?
4. Who makes contributions to the plan and in what amounts?
   You
   Employer
   Union dues
   Assessments
5. What is the normal retirement date of your plan?
6. Can you retire early? What reduction in benefits?
7. What are the vesting rules of the plan? When are you fully vested?
8. How many years toward vesting are you credited with so far?
9. What level of benefits can be projected for you based on your earnings and years of service?
10. Will there be a cost-of-living increase of payments?
11. Will there be survivor benefits?
12. What are the rules regarding pension benefits if you are terminated prior to retirement age?
13. How are pension benefits paid? Lump sum? Annuity?
14. What disability benefits are provided in the plan?
15. What is the financial health of the plan? Is it under-funded? Overfunded?
16. Are the benefits insured by the PBGC?

CHAPTER 11

THE WRONG SIDE OF FORTY

Don't give up on the idea of retiring early just because you are over 40. Sure, it's too late to make the goal of retiring at age 42, but why not aim for financial independence by 50 or 55. A tremendous amount can be accomplished in 10 to 15 years. The one big disadvantage you have is the shorter time span to save. Contrasting that are some major advantages.

THE ADVANTAGES

1. You are more disciplined in your ability to save and spend.
2. You have considerably more assets than when you were 25: equity in your home, a pension account that is vested, some savings, and so on.
3. Major purchases are behind you. Home formation is the most expensive period in a person's life. Mortgages are almost paid off.
4. You make more income now and more of it is discretionary.
5. College expenses may be upon you now, but soon that will be behind you.
6. Certain retirement plans permit you to put away a large amount of annual contribution because you have a shorter time to meet your goal.
7. If you retire at 55 to 60, you have fewer retirement years to save for than a very young person planning to retire at 40 to 45.

In fact, between the ages of 40 and 55, a person is in the peak earning years of his or her career. This is the period when *most* people begin to plan and save for retirement. Let's face it. Despite all the pleading to start retirement planning at age 30, how many do this? Very few. Most young people who are just getting started with their career, their marriage, and their family put retirement last on the list of their priorities. People who are in their late 20s or early 30s are immortal! Retirement is something to worry about when you are old—about age 40!

Thus, if you are 40 plus, don't despair. You are in the majority. Start with a thorough review of your retirement expectations to estimate your financial needs. Then, as suggested earlier, conduct an analysis to determine what amount of income you could generate from savings, sale of home, pension, IRAs, and so on at the time you retire early. Now the challenge is to save enough to be able to get there.

GREATER RETURNS CAN MAKE THE DIFFERENCE

As important as time is in the process of saving, the amount of interest you can earn or the growth rate in your equity is likewise important.

For example, if you invested $10,000 each year for 20 years at 5 percent interest, you would have $330,000 at the end of the period. But, if you could make your money compound at a 25 percent rate, you could have the same total after only 10 years. Or, if you could earn a more reasonable 10.5 percent yield, you would have as much after 15 years. A high return can make it happen for you a lot faster.

Gambling doesn't make sense in retirement planning. But an important element in saving smart, especially when time is limited, is to manage your money for the greatest return consistent with your tolerance for risk.

A SAMPLE PLAN

If you are age 40, how about this plan? You decide you will need an income of $50,000 a year at age 55, your target retirement date.

An evaluation of present assets reveals you have a net equity in your home of $275,000 and savings in financial assets of

$60,000. Your pension plan will pay you $45,000 a year at age 65 if you work until age 55, and you have IRAs now worth $22,000.

Value of Assets Now	Income Potential At 55	At 65
Home $275,000	?	?
Savings $60,000	?	?
Pension		$45,000/yr
IRAs $22,000	?	?

Home: At a conservative appreciation of 5 percent a year, your home would be worth $572,000 when you are age 55. If you assume you can find a nice smaller home or condo for half the value of the equity, you will have about half the value minus taxes of about 30 percent (remember the $125 thousand one-time exclusion).

Equity appreciation	$572,000
One-time exclusion	− 125,000
Basis (price paid for house)	− 149,000
	$298,000
Tax rate	.30
Owe	$89,400
Net equity minus tax	$482,600
Half remaining after condo purchase	$241,300

If you annuitize at 10 percent for the assumed 30 years of your remaining life expectancy, it can pay you about $25,000 a year.

Savings: If you can save an additional $10,000 a year between now and age 55 to add to your $60,000 in current savings, you would have a nice bundle. If these monies could grow at 10 percent tax deferred, you would have a nest egg of $568,000 at age 55. If the money can be tax-deferred in a 401k salary reduction plan or a self-employment Keogh, that is ideal. If not, consider purchasing an annuity or a single-premium life policy from an insurance company that will allow you to contribute annually and earn compound rates without annual taxes. A pool of money of $568 thousand can produce an annual income of $60,000 at 10 percent interest over 30 years.

IRAs: If you continue the maximum contribution of $4,000 a year for you and your working spouse, you will have $219,000 by age 55 if you can earn 10 percent. If you stop contributing at 55 but let the money build until age 65, you will then have $568,000. From age 65, this can produce an income of about $67,000 for the 20 years of life expectancy.

Using the two pools of money concept, you can retire at age 55 and have an income of $85,000 a year by selling your home, annuitizing the half less taxes, and buying a smaller home or condo outright for the other half. As noted, this will provide an annual income of $25,000. The balance comes from the income your savings generates which was calculated to be $60,000. At age 55, at 5 percent inflation, the $85,000 is equal to about $41,000 today.

Value of Assets at age 55		Income Potential at 55	at 65
Home	$241,300	$25,000	$25,000
Savings	$569,000	60,000	60,000
Pension			45,000
IRAs	$219,000		
	568,000 at 65	_____	67,000
		$85,000	$197,000

At age 55, your income would be $9,000 short of your goal of $50,000. You could make up the difference by part-time work. At age 65, your pension and IRA money kick in for an additional $112,000. Your total income would now be $197,000. At the 5 percent rate of inflation, this would be equal to $58,000 in today's dollars. Not bad. And, we have not even allowed for any Social Security payments.

Thus, by saving $10,000 a year plus the $4,000 in IRAs for the next 15 years, you can retire at 55. This example assumed a 10 percent compounded return. If you can earn 12 percent or even 15 percent, you will make the goal that much quicker.

CHAPTER 12

SPECIAL ISSUES FOR WOMEN AND SINGLES

It's not pleasant to discuss it, but it's true: men and women living alone have a tougher time trying to retire early. The system is biased against the single-person household. Their income is less, tax rates higher, and saving habits more difficult.

TWO CAN MAKE MORE THAN ONE

It is common sense that two incomes can be greater than one. However, household data reveal a larger gap than just two to one. The following Table and Figures document the much lower median income of women who live alone. While married couples have a median income of about $30,000, a female head without children under 18 makes $20,000. A female head with children under 18 has a median income of only $10,800, and the woman who truly lives alone (no family present), makes $9,700. The man in this live-alone situation makes $16,100. (See Table 12–1) Some of this can be explained by the older age of the live-alones. Much of it is simply due to women's lower earnings.

In a study by the Women's Research and Education Institute, "The American Woman 1987–1988," they found the median weekly earnings for women working full-time in 1987 were 70 percent of those enjoyed by men. The large salary disparity between men and women exists for all educational levels. Nevertheless, women have made progress in obtaining a larger portion of some better-paying professional jobs. (See Figure 12–1)

TABLE 12-1
Haves and Have Nots (1986 Households in Thousands, by Household Type and 1985 Income.)

	Families					Nonfamilies		
	Married Couples with Children <18 at Home	Married Couples without Children <18 at Home	Other Female Head with Children <18 at Home	Other Female Head without Children <18 at Home	Other Male Head	Men Living Alone	Women Living Alone	Other
All households.........	24,627	26,303	6,103	4,108	2,416	8,284	12,891	3,721
Under $10,000..........	1,609	2,478	2,898	867	403	2,570	6,579	376
$10,000 to $19,999.....	4,022	5,683	1,671	1,165	523	2,371	3,590	796
$20,000 to $29,999.....	5,219	5,213	876	877	578	1,624	1,736	758
$30,000 to $39,999.....	5,135	4,054	385	588	391	902	591	662
$40,000 to $49,999.....	3,476	3,037	145	298	210	364	203	480
$50,000 to $59,999.....	2,109	2,189	72	130	142	221	100	239
$60,000 to $74,999.....	1,597	1,735	34	101	77	100	54	223
$75,000 and over......	1,460	1,914	22	82	92	132	38	187
				Percent Distribution				
All Households........	100.0%	100.0%	100.0%	100.0%	100.0%	100.0%	100.0%	100.0%
Under $10,000..........	6.5	9.4	47.5	21.1	16.7	31.0	51.0	10.1
$10,000 to $19,999.....	16.3	21.6	27.4	28.4	21.6	28.6	27.8	21.4
$20,000 to $29,999.....	21.2	19.8	14.4	21.3	23.9	19.6	13.5	20.4
$30,000 to 39,999.....	20.9	15.4	6.3	14.3	16.2	10.9	4.6	17.8
$40,000 to $49,999.....	14.1	11.5	2.4	7.3	8.7	4.4	1.6	12.9
$50,000 to $59,999.....	8.6	8.3	1.2	3.2	5.9	2.7	.8	6.4
$60,000 to $74,999.....	6.5	6.6	.6	2.5	3.2	1.2	.4	6.0
$75,000 and over......	5.9	7.3	.4	2.0	3.8	1.6	.3	5.0
Median income........	$32,400	$29,400	$10,800	$20,100	$24,100	$16,100	$9,700	$28,700

Married couples with children have the highest median income. Women who live alone have the lowest.

Source: Thomas G. Exter, "Where the Money Is," *American Demographics*, March 1987, pp. 26-33.

FIGURE 12–1
Proportion of female workers in selected occupations, 1975 and 1985

	1975	1985
Architect	4.3%	11.3%
Bartender	35.2	47.9
Bus driver	37.7	49.2
Dentist	1.8	6.5
Elementary school teacher	85.4	84.0
Lawyer, judge	7.1	18.2
Mail carrier	8.7	17.2
Registered nurse	97.0	95.1
Waiter/waitress	91.1	84.0
Welder	4.4	4.8

Yearly earnings by sex and educational attainment of full-time
year-round worker. 1984 (in dollars).

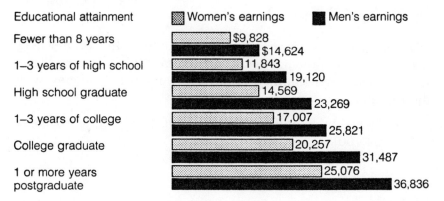

Source: U.S. Bureau of Census, U.S. Bureau of Labor Statistics.

TWO CAN SAVE MORE THAN ONE

"Two Can Save More Than One." This seemingly common sense
statement may be true for more reasons than you think. The
obvious reason is that a household with two incomes may have
more discretionary money to save for the future.

Another reason is that the government permits you to save
more in a variety of ways. Taxes are higher for singles for the

same level of income than they are for married couples. (See Figure 12–2) IRA limits are also higher. A single person can save a maximum of $2,000 a year. A two-income couple can shelter up to $4,000 a year. Even a couple where one spouse works and the other is essentially unemployed (makes less than $250) can contribute $2,250 a year—12.5 percent more than the limit of a single person.

These same differences carry over to pension plans where one person is limited by the cap on his or her defined benefit. Two people can save twice as much or more tax sheltered. Social Security is similar as well. Two previously working spouses may command a much greater benefit payment than one single person though his or her contributions may have been at the maximum through the years.

WOMEN AND MONEY

Women have fewer financial aspects than men. In a *Money* magazine survey of financial decision makers of 2,250 United States households, some findings regarding women and money were distressing:

- Women have half the financial assets of men ($26,900 vs. $54,700).

FIGURE 12–2
1988 Tax Rates

Tax Rate	Single	Married Filing Jointly and Quali- fying Widow(er)
15%	0–$17,850	0–$29,750
28%	over $17,850	over $29,750
Tax Rate	**Married Filing Separately**	**Head of Household**
15%	0–$14,875	0–$23,900
28%	over $14,875	over $23,900

- More women than men have less than $5,000 in savings (55 percent vs. 35 percent).
- Half of the women surveyed said they were uncomfortable with their standard of living.
- Twice as many women as men said they worry about money "very often" (31 percent vs. 15 percent).
- When they invest, women are more conservative. Only 22 percent own stocks or mutual funds vs. 43 percent of men.

WIDOWS AND WIDOWERS

Today, there are over 10 million widows in the United States. In fact, 9 of every 10 women will be widowed at some time in their lives. At age 60, only half of all women are living with their husbands.

Knowing the great odds that you will be a retired widow at some point, it is important to understand and plan an income stream for when the old boy is gone. Social Security and pension benefits are often cut when the retired husband passes away, leaving the widow to suffer. One answer is for younger married couples to plan now for what payments the wife will receive under the assumption of a deceased spouse. With more than half of women now working and contributing to household income, it is equally wise to estimate the husband's income in retirement if his wife were to die before he did.

DO IT FOR YOURSELF

It's not all bleak. There are some financial positives to being in a live-alone situation. If you are young and single, you can retire early with careful planning. The previous discusson almost sounds like a prescription to "find a mate." But that is not true. In fact, the worst thing you can do is to "do nothing" in anticipation that you will eventually marry and have someone take care of you. Many young women do this, but it can backfire. Divorces are so prevalent that many people who do marry later find themselves with a cash settlement but little or no retirement benefits after the divorce. Take care of yourself. Plan your future as if there were no one else who will do it for you.

If you are single and anticipate being so in the future, you must save to generate 60 to 80 percent of your working salary in order to retire young. For a person who has lived on a modest income during working years, this is possible with good saving and investment habits.

You do not face many expenses that families have: medical bills, clothing for kids, a large house, and college expenses. This means more money to sock away for later. But don't be too conservative in your investments. If you do not know how to invest, seek advice from a reputable brokerage firm or financial advisor. Remember the power of high returns and compound interest.

Another big difference between what marrieds and singles do: buying a house. In general, if you can afford it, do buy a house or condo rather than rent. Years of paying rent produces nothing of value. Home buying allows you to leverage your savings and it provides about the only tax shelter open to you. Since you can contribute only $2,000 to an IRA, home mortgages are the only big tax shelter a single person can get. The home is an investment, that at worst, keeps up with inflation and creates forced saving. If you can't discipline yourself to put away $1,000 or more a month, a mortgage can help you do it!

Also contribute the maximum to an IRA account. Some singles who are young with professional-level salaries above $25,000 and company pensions shun IRAs because they are told that not all of their contribution is tax deductible. This is true. But even if none of it were deductible, the interest accumulation is still tax deferred. Where else can you invest $2,000, choose your investment vehicle, and postpone any taxes until you withdraw the money maybe 30 years later. Remember, you will not be taxed on the nondeductible portions of your contributions. Even if you choose to withdraw it 10 years later and pay the 10 percent early withdrawal penalty, you will be ahead with the IRA.

CHAPTER 13

RETIRE YOUNG: 50 THINGS YOU CAN DO TO MAKE IT HAPPEN

Throughout the book, suggestions were made to help you realign your spending and saving habits, your retirement and pension accounts, and your vision of a lifestyle in early retirement.

To make certain that you are influenced to *act* as much as to dream, this chapter offers fifty things you can and should do to move toward your goal of retiring young. These actions are categorized in the following six prescriptions:

Set Retirement Goals
Manage Your Career For Lifetime Income
Structure a Retirement Plan
Control Spending
Save Smart
Use Retirement Tools

SET RETIREMENT GOALS

1. Set a concrete date as your goal for retiring. Whether you continue to work after that is irrelevant. Vague objectives are never met.
2. Be realistic in choosing your target date. Retiring young means different things to different people. To some 55 is young, to others it may be 40 or 45. If you set an

unrealistically young age, you may become discouraged and quit. If you select an age too far out in the future, you may lack motivation.

3. Make a list of all the things you will do when you can retire. Update the list over the years so that you keep the dream active.
4. During your working years, continuously sample what early retirement would be like. Spend some days off in the retirement location of your choice. Do the things you plan to do then. This will reinforce or clarify your goals and motivation.

MANAGE YOUR CAREER FOR LIFETIME INCOME

5. Draft a lifetime scenario of your working career. If you are in your 20s, 30s, or even 40s, talk to older peers in your profession to see what most of them do by age 55.
6. Never assume your company is loyal to you. Management or ownership can and does change. Think of your corporate employer as a consulting client, not a parent. Manage that consulting relationship to your best advantage.
7. Manage your career over the long-term for maximum income by taking jobs that will make you more valuable to someone else.
8. Don't stay in a job learning the same thing for too long. Move on if the company won't move you up.
9. Leverage what you learn with new companies or customers.
10. Consider starting your own company and prepare for it during your early career by learning something you can sell to many customers or clients—not just one employer!
11. Plan your career so that you will be able to have a source for outside income after you retire. This can supplement retirement income and make it easier to retire possibly earlier. Develop skills and contacts that will put you in demand for part-time or consulting work.

STRUCTURE A RETIREMENT PLAN

12. Calculate what amount of income you will need when you retire at your target age. Draft a scenario of what you plan to do with your "retirement years." Plan a life-simplification scenario where you can cut overhead and expenses.
13. Conduct a financial audit of your needs and means and have a life plan for what you will generate and what you will spend for periods of 15 years, such as from age 35 to 50, 50 to 65, and 65 to 80.
14. Think of having two pools of money for the retirement years. One pool for the early years of retirement when part-time working income is possible and another for when IRAs, pensions, and Social Security kick in.
15. Determine what financial targets you must meet in the year you retire and for every year between now and then.
16. Target to save enough to provide during retirement, 60 percent to 80 percent of your final working years income.
17. Be sure to calculate future retirement needs in future dollars, allowing for reasonable inflation.
18. To make early retirement easier, do not plan to leave a large estate to your heirs. Willingness to draw down principal during retirement permits saving a smaller nest egg to provide the same income stream.
19. Plan your retirement accommodations. Investigate moving to a less expensive area of the country.
20. Consider buying a retirement home as a second home when you are in your 30s or 40s. Pay off the house during your working years when tax brackets are higher. Take advantage of the "forced savings" as the retirement home appreciates with inflation.
21. Sell your primary residence after age 55 and receive up to $125,000 in capital appreciation free of taxes.
22. Monitor your performance every year relative to annual goals. This will allow you to alter your behavior if you fall behind in any year.

23. Get a professional financial advisor to help you plan your savings and retirement years.

CONTROL SPENDING

24. Break the work-and-spend cycle. Don't fall into the trap of "I worked hard to earn it, so I am going to spend it to reward myself." This guarantees the necessity of working until you die. Instead think: "I worked hard to earn it. I don't want to have to work this hard in the future."
25. Minimize credit purchases especially with high-rate credit cards.
26. Discipline yourself to keep credit balances under 10 percent of after-tax income.
27. Limit big-ticket installment debt items such as autos which can increase your total purchase cost 50 percent or more. If it won't fit in a one or two years' budget, it's too expensive to buy.
28. Minimize spending on intangibles and depreciating assets and shift more spending to potentially appreciating hard assets and financial assets.

SAVE SMART

29. Take advantage of the "geometric increases" of compound interest by starting to save at an early age.
30. Increase the percentage of income you dedicate to retirement savings as you get older. It is easier to save 15 percent to 20 percent or more as your discretionary income rises in middle age.
31. When you receive wage increases, increase your retirement contribution at least proportionately.
32. Treat lump-sum payments you receive during working years as saving opportunities, not windfalls. Salary bonuses, tax refunds, inheritances, and the like can be the

best pools of money to save since they are usually not counted on for paying expenses.

33. If you have a two-income household, try to live off of one and save the other.

34. Don't be *too* conservative in your investment decisions. An interest rate just 10 percent higher (e.g. 11 percent vs. 10 percent) could produce returns say after 25 years that are 25 percent higher.

35. Consider hobbies or interests with investment potential such as collectibles that can be converted to income producers at retirement.

36. Don't miss the opportunity to have "forced savings" through home ownership. This is especially true for singles who have few means of tax shelter and poor savings habits.

USE RETIREMENT TOOLS

37. Calculate expected Social Security benefits at your "normal retirement age" and at the early retirement age of 62. If you need help with this, contact your company's benefits office or the Social Security Administration. Look in the phone directory under United States Government, Health and Human Services Department, or Social Security Administration. You pay in every year; why not see what you will get back?

38. Let Uncle Sam contribute to your retirement by saving in tax-sheltered accounts.

39. Don't wait for your employer to tell you about pension options and retirement dates. Go to the benefits office and learn everything you can about what is offered and your options in the retirement plans. Participate as much as you can afford to.

40. Ask your employer to calculate future income projections at your target retirement age so you will know how much to expect. If your employer does not allow retirement payments at that age (e.g., at 45), ask for

an estimate of the vested-cash value you could expect to take if you left the company. At that time, you could choose a lump-sum distribution or an IRA rollover. Or, wait to withdraw the funds at age 65 using them for your long-term pool of money.

41. Take advantage of company retirement plans such as 401(k)s 403(b)s, SEPs, pensions, and the like.

42. Consider contributing to corporate retirement plans that are portable. Most company plans require you to be 65 to collect. Salary reduction plans such as 401(k)s can be rolled over into IRAs any time you choose to leave and retire.

43. Open an IRA for yourself (and your spouse). Contribute the maximum allowable and do it annually. Make your contribution at the start of each year.

44. Consider harvesting your IRA with annuity-type payments to avoid penalties if you need the income prior to 59 ½.

45. If you are near your target retirement age by 15 years or fewer and are self-employed, definitely investigate a defined-benefit Keogh plan.

46. If you have any self-employed income (even if you work for someone else full time), consider a Keogh plan.

47. Consider tax-deferred annuities or single-premium life policies as a way to capitalize on tax-free compounding if you have a pension fund with too low a limit.

48. If you are in high tax brackets, consider municipal bonds for tax-free compounding outside of retirement accounts.

49. Evaluate your insurance posture. If you have whole life, make sure that the investment component is carrying its weight relative to alternative non-insurance vehicles. Annuitize insurance cash values if any at your retirement.

50. Why work for one-half pay? Once your pension will pay you 50 percent or more of your income, you *may* be better off to quit and take a new job where you can earn more than half of your previous salary.

Chapter 14

HOW THEY DID IT: TEN WHO RETIRED YOUNG

To help broaden your perspective on how to retire young, ten case histories are presented revealing the variety of ways that people seek and reach the same goal. Some personal information has been modified to protect the identities of the individuals. Still, the basic facts are accurate.

Some avenues to achieve early retirement that are prevalent today did not exist twenty years ago. The individual retirement accounts were not available ten years ago. Some of the newer tools described in this book have become more effective as Congress changed the laws. In the 70s and earlier, real estate and various tax shelters were tools people used to invest and defer taxes. Thus, over time some saving and investment vehicles have been eliminated or made less effective while others have come on stream. This confirms the wisdom of constantly evaluating the tools you use in light of changes in the economy, tax laws, and your own financial circumstances.

These case histories illustrate many of the principles articulated in the previous chapters: long-term career planning, starting young, dedication to goals, lifestyle simplification after retirement, use of expert counselors, diligent saving, saving smart with retirement tools, two pools of money, and a variety of other ideas and techniques.

If they did it, you can do it. There is no magic or luck in these stories. Most people manage a comfortable retirement without either. So there is every reason to believe that if you follow the same practices you *can* retire young.

PAUL AND CHRIS SAFTLER

Paul and Chris Saftler of Danbury, Connecticut were already married 14 years when Paul began to talk of early retirement. He was 36 and still moving ahead as an advertising account executive. His concern for the future stemmed from an observation that "advertising is a young person's business." He had seen his career advance when the company promoted him to the position of his former boss who was let go. The man was only 57 and never did find another job in the advertising field. Paul's promotion led to a depression. "Why will I be any different at that age? I better be set by the time I reach 50 or I will be vulnerable, too."

Chris was a high school teacher, but she did not work in education while their three children were growing up. Only two years younger than Paul, Chris was working for a private school at the time Paul suggested they work to retire by age 50. With only 14 years until that target date, Paul and Chris decided to make their mark by buying and holding some apartments. With the strong cash flow of over $60,000 from their two jobs, they purchased a piece of rental real estate about every three years. By age 45, they had rental property worth $450,000 with a positive cash flow of $21,000 a year. With five years to go, the Saftlers opened a (at the time) new IRA account for each of them. Pension dollars were building up also. Chris had a 403(b) plan which she funded to the maximum. It would be worth about $43,000 when she was 48. Paul's agency had a profit-sharing plan and a stock-option plan. By continuing his contribution until age 50, it would be enough to pay him $37,000 a year when he turned 60.

For the next five years, the Saftlers saved as much as they could. College expenses precluded further real estate purchases. When he turned 50, they retired. Their home was quite valuable, but they had paid it off so they stayed put. They left their retirement accounts alone to be used for the later years after 60. Current income consisted of $28,000 of rental income, and $12,000 a year from a savings pool of $77,000 they intended to draw down until he reached 60. At that time, the pension and IRA money would be used. They planned to wait until 65 to start Social Security to maximize its payments later in their lives.

The Saftlers adjusted well to their new lifestyle. Chris had felt burned out some years before they quit. "I was ready to do something—anything different." Paul's advertising career had plateaued. "I was not ready to quit, but any advancement was no longer possible." The Saftlers are now continuing to buy low-priced fixer-upper real estate. Using the skill they developed from earlier real estate investing, they now work at this new business with dedication, but without pressure. "We wanted the freedom to do what we want at the pace we want. That's just what we are doing now."

BEN AND MARGE FRYER

Ben and Marge Fryer never had an extravagant lifestyle. Their Jackson, Mississippi home was modest, and the Fryers had two small cars. Ben was a planning manager for the state and Marge was a secretary for a small furniture business. The one thing the Fryers did spend money on was travel. Marge said they met while on a bicycle trip around the state. "It's what we live for. Ben wants to plan a new trip as soon as we return from an earlier one. Our work schedules prevent us from going to many places that are a little too far away for a weekend jaunt."

At age 32, Ben had complained of the confinement of working. It was Marge who suggested they save and quit so they could travel when and where they wanted to. The Fryer's combined salary was under $40,000 in today's dollars when they were in their 30s, but they believed they could retire young because they intended to have no children. Although they had no formal plan or target retirement date, they dreamed of leaving their jobs by the time they were 45. This didn't happen, but they did pack it in when Ben was 52. His state retirement plan would provide 72 percent of his final-year income at age 62, as he had 31 years employment with the state.

A slow-build savings plan was the major focus of their plan to stop working and start traveling. For the first few years, the

Fryers simply contributed to their bank savings account. Fortunately, a neighbor who was an insurance agent convinced them to diversify and purchase annuity contracts. These allowed the savings to compound tax free and guarantee fixed payments beginning when Ben turned 55.

With savings in a mutual fund worth $118,000, Ben felt comfortable to retire at 52. The savings could tide them over until their annuity payments began when he was 55. They are counting on four sources of their future income: interest income from the mutual fund savings, annuity payments, pension income from the state plan due when he is 62, and her Social Security drawable in the same year.

The couple has only recently quit their jobs. "We have so much time now, we plan trips constantly. Although our income is less than when we both were working, we have no other real expenses except eating and touring. Our next purchase will be a small RV."

CATHY DONAHUE

Cathy Donahue grew up in a suburb of Boston. Her father was a fireman and worked until age 60. It was her uncle who made a lasting impression on her. "He was never really wealthy, but he somehow saved enough to retire in his forties." While my father complained every day about his obligations, my Uncle Mickey seemed to have none." Cathy knew in high school that Uncle Mickey was her role model. After graduating in 1960, she entered Boston University and eventually received an MBA from Michigan. When she graduated in 1967, she took a job as a sales and marketing trainee with a large computer company. When her career stalled there four years later, she moved on to another firm. By 1979, she had worked for four different employers, but she was assistant director of marketing for her current employer.

All this moving precluded any vesting of pension benefits, but Cathy had made up for it by consistent saving and investment. She owned three small houses valued then at $234,000, had a savings account worth $37,000, and a nice German car costing $16,000. "I was saving everything I could then, but my life wasn't bad. I bought as much as any of my friends; I just bought different things."

Sensing she could achieve her goal of being financially independent, she consulted a financial advisor. He set up a plan for her to save $15,000 a year (27 percent of her salary) for 7 years. She put $2,000 in an IRA, $5,000 in annuities, and $5,000 in a stock mutual fund. In 1986, her property was worth $447,000. her annuities would now pay $4,600 a month. The stock mutual fund was worth $81,000. The IRA account was worth $17,000. Her net worth was $483,000.

Cathy did not retire in 1987 as she had intended. Her salary has risen and she is still saving. "I thought it would be great to retire and I guess I could, but I will keep working until I get tired of it. The good thing is that I know I can do what I want to. My boss seems to know that. I work hard, but he doesn't push me around. Maybe I will quit in a couple of years."

DICK AND CHARLENE ROBINSON

Dick Robinson began his career in the oil fields of Texas. By age 47, he was a high-level executive for a major oil company. The Robinsons had two children and Charlene spent most of her time being a homemaker and mother.

During a summer vacation, Dick and Charlene fell in love with Naples, Florida. They bought a second home there and travelled to Naples whenever they could. Dick was an avid golfer.

Before Dick reached his 50th birthday, he had a vision: "I am going to die in my office. In a dream I had, I never made it to retirement in Naples. When I fell dead on top of my desk, my boss came in and told everyone in the office that he now owned my condo in Naples and to visit him there! That was it." Dick asked his accountant to prepare a plan for how he could get out in 5 years or less.

The Robinsons had a lot of money, but their cost of living was also high—over $150,000 a year. The accountant told Dick there was no way unless he did two things—save a lot of his income and reduce his cost of living. By selling their family home in Dallas, the Robinsons could net over $385,000. With the tax exemption, he was able to avoid tax on $125,000 if he waited until age 55 to sell. He could pay off the Florida condo and have $210,000 left.

If Dick retired at 55, his pension would be just 58 percent of what it would have been if he kept working until 62. Still, he believed that the pension and his Social Security (Charlene never worked outside the home) would be sufficient at age 62—about $37,000.

The problem was how to have enough income to live on between age 55 and 62. The accountant suggested that Dick become an aggressive saver between ages 50 and 55. Dick's goal was $50,000 a year. The sacrifice meant no big purchase for 5 years. During that time, Dick bought conservative stocks and bonds with the goal of some capital appreciation to shift money toward the years after age 55 when his tax bracket might be lower.

At 55, Dick's portfolio was worth $311,000. He and Charlene left Dallas and moved into their Naples, Florida condo. It has been 2 years since then. "It has been more difficult than I thought adjusting to a lower income. Even the low level of inflation we have now is eroding my income. We can easily get by on what we have, but I want more. So I'm looking for part-time work or maybe a small business to get into. I play golf every day. It's a great life."

LEON AND SHELLY COHEN

Leon Cohen never intended to retire early, but when he got the chance he was prepared. Growing up in a working-class neighborhood in Chicago, Leon saw his father live from paycheck to paycheck. "When I married Shelly, I told her I never wanted to be constantly broke like my father. We are going to live within our means."

Leon worked for a number of companies as a salesman before he was 21. Then he went to work for a large chemical company in Baltimore. When he left at age 53, he had worked 32 years for that firm. In a restructuring, Leon received an early retirement offer that he didn't want. "I wasn't ready to leave. I'm a young man. But Shelly said: What future will you have there if you don't go now that they've asked you. Fortunately, I could afford to take the offer. It would have been terrible if I had to stay."

Leon and Shelly were disciplined savers all of their working lives. Shelly held various jobs with the newspaper while their children were growing up. She saved most of her take-home pay and invested it in savings bonds. Some years the returns were modest, but the principal was safe. Leon had saved more than 10 percent of his gross salary every year since they married. Like Shelly, a conservative investor, he had put most of these funds in balanced mutual funds. "I look back and know we could have lived more high on the hog if we had spent all of our income. But now my neighbors are envious. They all complain that their new bosses are yuppies who know nothing, but still run their lives. I don't have to answer to anyone anymore."

The early retirement package Leon received offered a severance of one year's pay and pension retirement benefits at 62 that were equal to what he would have gotten if he had stayed working until age 60.

At age 53, he had 9 years to support himself until these pension monies and Social Security would begin. The Cohens total savings were $566,000, paying interest income of about $43,000. Using the severance pay, Leon paid off his mortgage. He converted some of his mutual funds to higher-yield bond income in the second year when his tax rates were lower. The Cohens say they are doing nicely on $52,000.

WARREN AND BARBARA BROWNING

Warren and Barbara met while working at a large West Coast bank. They had both received their MBA and were financial analysts. In the late 70s, they moved to New York City to enhance their careers by working with more sophisticated firms. After two years in New York, the pace began to take a toll on their marriage. Barbara was traveling every week and saw Warren only on weekends. The glamor of the two-professional-household lifestyle was wearing thin. Warren missed the West Coast so they decided to move to California after quitting their jobs. "It was risky. After making a down payment on a house, we had

$11,000 left in savings. We didn't know how to do anything else except finance. We did make a lot of contacts in New York and in Los Angeles, so we decided to start our own financial consulting company."

The company got off to a good start, but Warren complained that the work was just "more of the same." He said he wanted to work harder, make and save more, and get out as early as possible. This led to a 10-year plan for retirement. "Well, we had a good plan, but the IRS was siphoning off all of our income." A lawyer suggested contacting a pension plan advisor. This advisor set up a defined-benefit Keogh plan. "This was one of the smartest moves we ever made. We were able to save half of our income in this pension plan. With the other half, we saved what was left after taxes and bought tax-free municipal bonds." The couple also contributed $4,000 a year to IRAs. In some years, the business generated almost $500,000 a year.

After eight years, the couple was again burned-out and ready for change. Barbara wanted to do something different. They decided to retire two years earlier than originally planned.

Their municipal bond and personal savings income had risen to almost $70,000. The Keogh plans were closed and rolled over into IRAs. This savings invested in zero coupon treasuries, will be worth almost three million when Warren turns 59 1/2. The couple simplified their lifestyle by selling their home in Los Angeles and buying one in a nearby retirement community that cost a third as much. Warren said, "It is scary to retire when you are in your 40s and have to plan your financial future for 35 to 45 years. We have savings for the near term and longer term, but who knows what we will need 30 years from now? I don't worry though. We are enjoying the free time while we are younger."

MARIA GLASS

Maria Glass is now 48 years old and still lives in the town where she was born—Albany, New York. She works as a dental assistant in the office of a local dentist. She has never married. By the time she was 35 she began saving for her future. Maria's older cousin never married and had to work as a nurse until she was 68 just to pay the bills. Maria decided she would be out from under financial pressure by age 55.

Ms. Glass became a homeowner at 37 and she traded up twice to her present home worth about $135,000. She has made a contribution to an IRA for six years. Her employer has a defined-contribution Keogh which she participates in.

Maria believes she will need an income of at least $18,000 to retire at 55. With seven years left to save, she needs to save only $6,200 a year to have a total capital of $184,000 available to generate the income she needs.

"During the years I have worked, my salary has risen from $11,000 to my current $28,000. I am used to living frugally. If I quit at 55, I will have to live on a fixed income for a long time. Maybe I will leave Albany and see what it is like somewhere else."

ALEX AND BARBARA DENBERG

At age 39, Alex Denberg got fired from his job as a financial officer of a large savings and loan in Nashville. The Denbergs had two small children and Barbara had not worked for 6 years. This trauma led Alex to focus on how he could achieve financial independence. The Denbergs had a conservative lifestyle, but they had only $73,000 in savings and a $55,000 equity in a $185,000 home.

Alex estimated that he would need $750,000 to be independent enough to not need an employer. Alex considered becoming self-employed, but he felt his personality and temperament was best suited to working for someone else and drawing a paycheck.

After four months, Alex was working again for another savings bank but this time with a different attitude. "I liked my new job, but I didn't trust any company. You have to look out for yourself."

The Denbergs planned to achieve their financial goals by using Alex's salary to buy real estate. Their first move was a trade up to a home in the $250,000 range. At the time, real estate was depressed in Nashville so this bought quite a house.

In 2 years, when property began to move up in price, the couple traded up again to a house priced over $375,000. As an executive of the bank, Alex got favorable financing rates which made the jump easier. After two-and-a-half years, they sold this house for $435,000 and bought a huge ranch on 35 acres for $580,000. The location was out of town, but in the path of progress. Barbara said this type of investing had other benefits as well. "The kids had a lot of space, we had wonderful homes, and they made money for us while we slept!"

Alex's career was progressing well. He was made a senior vice president and his future seemed assured. Three years later, Alex quit his job to the surprise of his peers. He sold their ranch for over $800,000 and the couple moved to Little Rock, Arkansas. The Denbergs have an income of $65,000 from their investments. Alex and Barbara have just started a small business—a toy store in a local mall. They have high hopes for the venture.

DAVID SPIRES

David Spires is now 51. He hasn't yet retired, but he could. David grew up in a large family and never had the opportunity to go to college. He built up a small business of newspaper deliverers before he was 25. He then moved to Los Angeles. With the money he had saved from his business he bought a defunct car wash. The business had been closed for over 2 years. After six months, David gave up and sold this business to a local businessman—at a loss. Using his knowledge of car washing, he went into a partnership with a relative and they bought a self-service car wash. This is one of those businesses where a lot of quarters can add up to thousands of dollars.

Since this business required no employees (David did all the maintenance and clean-up), a second car wash was soon purchased. By age 36, David owned a string of 9 car washes and became a millionaire. A disastrous divorce, however, forced him to sell 6 of them and he was wiped out at age 39. Vowing to rebuild his fortune and retire by 50, David sold the remaining car washes and moved to Fresno, California. "This was the only business I knew. But I had learned it well so I was sure I could do it again."

The market for this do-it-yourself car washing was undeveloped in this town so David had to proceed slowly. He bought one existing car wash for $110,000. He put up $25,000 and the owner carried the paper for the balance over 10 years. This one was a real money-maker and provided the capital to build two more with the bank's help.

By age 46, David owned seven car washes in Fresno and nearby towns. These businesses provided him with an income of over $200,000. To assure his retirement he opened a defined-contribution account for himself through the corporation he had established. In addition, the corporation makes payments on a life insurance policy on him which accumulates value which he can borrow against in his later years.

At 51, he still has not retired and is considering buying another car wash! But, he doesn't have to worry now about his future. "I thought I would quit when I had enough money. But what would I do? The only thing I've ever done is wash cars. So I'll stay with it. Now it's fun. I may even get married again."

DOUGLAS AND MAUREEN NORBE

The Norbes retired in 1986 on an income of $17,000. Eight years earlier, Maureen had a major operation for cancer. Doug said because be almost lost her, he wasn't going to waste time. They had had a lifelong dream of moving to Canada. They visited Vancouver whenever they could and imagined a life there.

Doug owned a small automotive garage and felt he could work anywhere. But Maureen was employed by the State of Oklahoma and she had a very good income. When they were in their 30s, they believed if they left Oklahoma, they would not be able to make as much money. By age 35, their combined income was $66,000. As most young people do, they spent most of the money they earned.

After 1978, when Maureen had her operation, the couple decided to save as much and as fast as possible. "We could not retire wealthy. We would still be working if we had not scaled back our cost of living. I knew we could make it on as little as $12,000 a year. When you live in a small town and don't commute to work, you save a bundle."

During the eight years between 1978 and 1986, the Norbes did two things to make their early retirement possible. They lived on Doug's income from the garage and saved all of Maureen's. Over eight years, this added up to $176,000. The money was invested by a stockbroker in a mix of stocks, bonds, and Ginnie Maes. The second thing they did was to buy a second house in the Vancouver area. By the time they moved there permanently, they only owed $29,000.

When the Norbes committed to move, they sold the auto garage and used the proceeds to pay off their house in Canada and to buy two annuities for each of them payable when they turn 65.

Doug is now 51 and the family must get by on the $17,000 until he turns 62 and can collect Social Security. They have no other funds to help them during this 11-year period. Doug is considering doing auto tune-ups in his garage. A little outside income would close the gap. "With no mortgage payments, Social Security deductions, or heavy State taxes, $17,000 goes a long way. Maybe as much as $30,000 in our working days in Oklahoma."

READINGS

Articles:

"Financial Planners—Fads, Frauds or Finds," *Self,* (October 1987), pp. 60–77.

"Taxes for Young Retirees," *Forbes,* (April 27, 1987), pp. 71–73.

"Early Retirement: Boon or Bust?," *Barron's,* (January 26, 1987), pp. 40–41.

Richard Elsberry, "Set Free," *The New York Times Magazine,* (January 4, 1987).

Elizabeth M. Fowler, "The Early Retirement Programs," *The New York Times,* (April 25, 1984).

Mary J. Rudie, "Plan for Retirement," *Restaurant Business,* (May 1, 1987).

Bickford Henchey, "Early Retirement May Lead to Lucky Break," *WSJ,* (November 3, 1986).

Marilyn Much, "Is Early Retirement Your Cup of Tea?" *Industry Week,* (November 10, 1986).

Richard Eisenberg and Wendy Lubetkin, "The Best Financial Planners . . . They're Masters of Budgeting, Investing, Taxes and Retirement." *Money, Special Issue,* (Fall 1987), p. 139.

"Early Retirement—Could You Pull It Off," *Changing Times,* (February 1984), pp. 26–31.

Larry Reibstein, "AT&T Study Shows Early Retirees Share a Range of Character Traits," *WSJ,* (September 4, 1987), p. 1, section 2.

Bradley Hitchings, "Packing It In Before 65," *Business Week,* (June 24, 1985), pp. 134–36.

Mark McCain, "Early Retirement: A Time For Late Bloomers," *50 Plus,* (September 1985), pp. 42–46.

Ann Finlayson, "The Lure of Early Retirement," *MacLeans,* (February 4, 1985), pp. 40–41.

USA Today, "Retirees Increasingly Well Off," "Workers Rejecting Incentives to Stay on The Job," (April 1987), pp. 15–16.

Janet Bamford, "Hang Tough Or Take The Gold Watch Early?," *Forbes,* (May 5, 1986), pp. 158–159.

"Here's Another Good Excuse To Retire Early," *Changing Times,* (March 1986), pp. 83–86.

Sarah Button White, "Investing For Early Retirement—Just In Case," *Money,* (March 1986), pp. 209–210.

Ronald Alsop, "As Early Retirement Grows In Popularity, Some Have Misgivings," *WSJ,* (April 22, 1984).

Robert McNatt, "An Early Retirement Is The Goal of Two Young Floridians," *Money,* (April 1985), pp. 39–42.

Peter Philipps, "Why Early Retirement May Not Work For You," *Business Week,* (May 11, 1987), p. 166.

Carey W. English, "Dropping Out: Why More Men Retire Early," *U.S. News & World Report,* (July 2, 1984), pp. 69–70.

Books:

AARP, *Looking Ahead, How to Plan Your Successful Retirement,* (Glenview, Ill.: Scott Foresman, 1987).

AARP, *Think of Your Future, Preretirement Planning Workbook,* (Glenview, Ill.: Scott Foresman, 1984).

Allan Fromme, AARP, *Life After Work, Planning It, Living It, Loving It,* (Glenview, Ill.: Scott Foresman, 1984).

Peter Weaver and Annette Buchanan, AARP, *What To Do With What You've Got,* (Glenview, Ill.: Scott Foresman, 1984).

Fred Nauheim, AARP, *239 Ways To Put Your Money To Work,* (Glenview, Ill.: Scott Foresman, 1986).

Michael Sumichrast, Ronald G. Shafer and Marika Sumichrast, AARP, *Planning Your Retirement Housing,* (Glenview, Ill.: Scott Foresman, 1984).

Peter A. Dickinson, AARP, *Sunbelt Retirement,* (Glenview, Ill.: Scott Foresman, 1986).

Peter A. Dickinson, AARP, *Retirement Edens,* (Glenview, Ill.: Scott Foresman, 1987).

Lawrence J. Kaplan, *Retiring Right, Planning For Your Successful Retirement,* (Wayne, N.J.: Avery Publishing Group, 1987).

J. K. Lasser, *All You Should Know About IRA, Keogh, and Other Retirement Plans,* (Englewood Cliffs, N.J.: J. K. Lasser Tax Institute, Prentice Hall, 1987).

William E. Donoghue, *Donoghue's Investment Tips For Retirement Savings,* (New York: Harper & Row, 1987).

Adriane G. Berg, *Your Wealth Building Years,* (New York: Newmarket Press, 1987).

Gerald Krefetz, *All About Saving,* (New York: John Wiley & Sons, 1987).

Frank Sacks, Siri Campbell, and Cameron Stauth, *The New IRA Handbook,* (Chicago: MCI Publishing, 1986).

Jeffrey A. Stern, *How To Become Financially Independent Before You're 35,* (Boston: Little, Brown and Co., 1986).

Arthur Young & Company, *The Arthur Young Preretirement Planning Book,* (New York: John Wiley & Sons, 1985).

Brian J. Sheen, *Nest Egg Investing,* (New York: G. P. Putnam's Sons, 1987).

Ray Vicker, *The Dow Jones-Irwin Guide To Retirement Planning,* (Homewood, Ill.: Dow Jones-Irwin, 1985).

David and Holly Franke, *Safe Places For The 80's,* (New York: The Dial Press, Doubleday, 1984).

Richard Boyer, David Savageau, *Rand McNally Places Rated Retirement Guide,* (Chicago: Rand McNally, 1983).

Paul Hirsch, *Pack Your Own Parachute,* (Reading, MA.: Addison-Wesley, 1987).

Nancy Dunnan, *Dun & Bradstreet's Guide to $Your Investments$ 1988,* (New York: Harper and Row, 1988).

Michael J. Boskin, *Too Many Promises,* (Homewood, Ill.: Dow Jones-Irwin, 1986).

INDEX